D0651994

PAST
CARING

A History of U.S.
Preschool Care and Education
for the Poor, 1820-1965

by

Emily D. Cahan

With a Foreword by
Bettye M. Caldwell

National Center for Children in Poverty
School of Public Health
Columbia University

JAMES P. ADAMS
LIBRARY
NO LONGER THE PROPERTY OF
RHODE ISLAND COLLEGE LIBRARY
RHODE ISLAND COLLEGE

Copies of this book are available for $5.95 each from the National Center for Children in Poverty, Columbia University, 154 Haven Avenue, New York, NY, 10032, 212-927-8793; FAX: 212-927-9162.

The National Center for Children in Poverty was initiated to strengthen programs and policies for the five million children under six and their families who live in poverty in America. The Center assesses past and present public and private sector initiatives in the areas of early education and child care, maternal and child health, and social support to poor families. The Center was established with generous core support from the Ford Foundation and the Carnegie Corporation of New York.

Copyright © 1989 by the National Center for Children in Poverty

All rights reserved.

Library of Congress Cataloging-in-Publication Data:

Cahan, Emily D., 1956-
   Past caring.

   Bibliography: p. 51.
   1. Education, Preschool—United States—History—19th century. 2. Education, Preschool—United States—History—20th century. 3. Socially handicapped children—Education (Preschool)—United States—History—19th century. 4. Socially handicapped children—Education (Preschool)—United States—History—20th century. 5. Day care centers—United States—History—19th century. 6. Day care centers—United States—History—20th century. I. Title.
LB1140.23.C34 1989   372.21'0973   89-3425
ISBN 0-926582-00-3

CONTENTS

NATIONAL CENTER FOR CHILDREN IN POVERTY

PANEL ON EARLY CHILDHOOD PROGRAMS

J. Lawrence Aber, Assistant Professor, Department of Psychology, Barnard College

Gordon M. Ambach, Executive Director, Council of Chief State School Officers

Helen F. Blank, Director, Child Care Division, Children's Defense Fund

*Barbara B. Blum, President, Foundation for Child Development

Barbara T. Bowman, Director of Graduate Studies, Erikson Institute

Bettye M. Caldwell, Donaghey Distinguished Professor of Education, Center for
Research on Teaching and Learning, University of Arkansas at Little Rock

Eugene E. Garcia, Chairman, Board of Studies in Education, University of California

Robert Greenstein, Director, Center on Budget and Policy Priorities

Sophia Bracey Harris, Executive Director, Federation for Child Care Centers of Alabama

Cheryl D. Hayes, Executive Director, National Commission on Children

Sharon Lynn Kagan, Associate Director, Yale Bush Center in Child Development and
Social Policy, Yale University

Sheila Kamerman, Professor and Department Chair, School of Social Work,
Columbia University

Alicia S. Lieberman, Associate Professor, Infant-Parent Program, San Francisco
General Hospital

Ruth W. Massinga, Chief Executive, The Casey Family Program

Anne W. Mitchell, Project Director, Public School Early Childhood Study, Bank Street
College of Education

Deborah A. Phillips, Assistant Professor, Department of Psychology, University of
Virginia

Mary Lou deLeon Siantz, Assistant Professor, Graduate Department of
Psychiatric/Mental Health Nursing, Indiana University School of Nursing

Patricia Siegal, Executive Director, California Child Care Resource and Referral
Network

Margaret Beale Spencer, Associate Professor, Division of Education Studies,
Emory University

Nancy E. Travis, Executive Director, Southern States Program, Save the Children
Foundation

David P. Weikart, President, High/Scope Educational Research Foundation

Caroline Zinsser, Director, Child Care Policy Study, Center for Public Advocacy Research

---

* Chair, Council of Advisors, Council Representative to Panel

PREFACE

Emily Cahan's historical review painstakingly underscores America's lack of commitment to providing high quality early childhood care and education for poor children. We have known for at least two centuries that the well-being of children from whatever background depends on caregiving that not only ensures their health and safety but also responds to their developmental needs. Yet we have failed to act systematically and boldly on that knowledge in the public policy arena.

During the 19th and early 20th centuries, two tiers of early childhood programs evolved in the United States. One tier, rooted in the social welfare system, was driven by a desire to reduce welfare payments—with scant attention to the needs of the child. This system of custodial "group child care" for low-income families was in sharp contrast to the second tier—child care rooted in the education system that provided "preschool education," mainly for children of the middle and upper-middle classes.

After World War II, a steady expansion of public kindergarten programs began to challenge this two-tiered system. Head Start arrived in the 1960s, followed in the 1970s by proposals for federal child care standards and expanded child care subsidies for low-income families. These decades promised progress toward high quality care and education for young children of all ages and backgrounds.

But public policy reversed this trend in the 1980s. Federal child care standards were not implemented, and funding for subsidized child care diminished.

As we begin the final decade of this century, do we at last have the political will to set things right?

Today, conservatives and liberals alike are paying unprecedented attention to the needs of low-income children and families for more and better early care and education. Several forces have encouraged this attentiveness. First, the rapid influx of married middle-class women with young children into the paid labor force has created a new and powerful constituency that favors governmental initiatives to increase the affordability, availability, and quality of child care services. Second, high quality early childhood programs for poor and minority children are now widely perceived as a way to break the cycle of poverty and build the human capital we need to maintain this nation's economic leadership into the next century.

Third, our disillusionment with the welfare system and a recently voiced sentiment—that welfare mothers must work if their middle-class counterparts have to—has prompted a new social policy requiring many on welfare to work.

While we are heartened by the public and political debates on the needs of low-income children and families, there is no commitment as yet to make the necessary public financial investment. Welfare reform, which mandates that mothers be trained and go to work, only guarantees subsidized child care services during the training period and for the first twelve months of employment. Moreover, no safeguards have been articulated to assure continuity of care for the child once this transitional period is over. Also, welfare reform does nothing to assure a poor family's access to high quality child care or to education for pre-school-age children. Other proposed legislation would increase child care subsidies to low-income families in general, and would boost modest efforts to improve the quality of available care. However, there is no indication at present that sufficient dollars will be appropriated to truly dismantle the two-tiered system we inherited—a system that has always been a disservice to our most vulnerable families and that creates long-term costs we cannot afford.

In the foreword to this monograph, Bettye Caldwell reminds us of Santayana's caution: "Those who cannot remember the past are condemned to repeat it." The National Center for Children in Poverty commissioned this volume because we believe that lessons from the past can and must inform the present. As policymakers and program administrators at all levels of government struggle to meet America's burgeoning demands for child care and education services, it is imperative that they not repeat or sustain failed policies. Rather, they must work to ensure high quality care and education for all children, built on our strong scientific research knowledge base that insists on quality in order to achieve progress.

I want to thank Emily D. Cahan for her thoughtful analysis and her grasp of the significant issues in the development of early childhood programs. I also wish to thank Bettye M. Caldwell for her astute and stimulating foreword, which is particularly pertinent because of her singular contributions to this field. Many others have participated in the preparation of this volume, including Center staff and the Center's Panel on Early Childhood Programs, whose comments were especially helpful in the early stages of the project. Their efforts are very much appreciated.

Judith E. Jones, Director
National Center for Children in Poverty

FOREWORD

Prologue to the Past

Bettye M. Caldwell

That the past is prologue is part of our vernacular. But that the early childhood movement even had a past does not always seem to be part of the thinking of some people. It is both amusing and shocking to talk to someone who has just "discovered" early childhood programs and who, in the excitement of that discovery, proclaims the power of the field to solve the high school dropout problem, wipe out drug addiction, and reduce the welfare rolls.

To these new converts, the field has no history. It began when they discovered it, and it earns its credibility from their endorsement. And yet, as is obvious from this brief but thorough history of the growth of the early childhood movement, the field has a dramatic and distinguished history. Emily Cahan has done a superb job of condensing the major events of that history. She introduces us to the people who provided the underlying concepts upon which programs were based or who undertook the difficult and sometimes delicate advocacy efforts that were necessary to gain public acceptance and support.

What strikes the reader most poignantly upon reading Cahan's history is how contemporary everything sounds. Compare, for example, the following quotes:

> By this means many of you, mothers of families, will be enabled to earn a better maintenance or support for your children; you will have less care and anxiety about them; while the children will be prevented from acquiring any bad habits, and gradually prepared to learn the best.

> Head Start will reach out to one million young children lost in a gray world of poverty and neglect, and lead them into the human family.

The first quote, dated 1816, is found in Cahan's history and is attributed to Robert Owen, the great Scottish proponent of early care and education. The second is from a 1965 newspaper clipping and is attributed to Lady Bird

Johnson, Honorary Chair of Head Start during its early years. A century and a half separates the statements, but the rhetoric is interchangeable.

It is the current relevance of Cahan's history that makes it so useful and so exciting. The social needs she documents as having helped generate early childhood services in the 19th century are still very much with us. We still have people living in poverty across several generations. We still have inequality of opportunity for development and education—inequality that seems to enhance the likelihood of success in life for those with adequate social and economic resources and to weaken the prospects of comparable success for those whose life histories lack these resources. And now, both absolutely and relatively, there are far more mothers who need child care support because they have young children and work outside the home.

The Future

From Cahan's history, at least three major generalizations can be drawn about the future of early childhood programs:

1. The field has always been conflicted about the potential benefits and risks its activities entail. Belief in the importance of the learning that occurs during the first years of life is not an idea that originated in the mid-20th century, Hunt and Bloom notwithstanding.* From the dawn of the 19th century, there were scientists and educators who perceived the plasticity of the child during the first few years of life and who saw education as the most likely means of improving an individual's life prospects. Such education was seen as making up for shortcomings in religious teaching by parents, as helping to form character, and as preventing crime and venality. At the same time, Cahan points out that opponents (and possibly proponents in unguarded moments) feared the spread of such ideas as invading the domain of the family and as possibly violating natural and religious laws. And, she notes, there were also those who feared the social unrest that might be generated by supplying evidence that one could move out of one's class.

These concerns about the "family-weakening" capacity of early childhood programs were echoed in 1971, when President Richard Nixon vetoed the first Comprehensive Child Development Act. They were echoed again in 1981 during the White House Conference on Families—echoed in tones that were often so loud that the scheduled speakers could not be heard in the cacophony. Having lived through that conflict, I found it especially enlightening to learn from Cahan that the field has never been free of it.

---

* See Hunt, J. M. (1961). *Intelligence and experience.* New York: Ronald Press; Bloom, B. (1964). *Stability and change in human characteristics.* New York: Wiley.

Whatever the validity of these concerns, then or now, surely they have brought about some good for families. It is interesting to note that concern about deleterious effects of early day nurseries was cited as one of the justifications for the passage of early legislation establishing the Aid to Dependent Children program (now called Aid to Families with Dependent Children). Recently, in what is surely an ironic twist of history, concern about the inadequacies of that program, about its intergenerational entrapment, and about its failure to reduce prolonged dependency has led to a renewed call for quality early childhood programs. Such services are being touted as essential for any meaningful welfare reform, with little or no concern about possible harm to either the children or their families. The programs are seen as promising double-edged benefits. On the one hand, they will provide the child with care and protection that will allow mothers either to work or to undergo training. At the same time, it is hoped they will start the children on the path to a level of future academic competence that will enable them to escape continued dependency.

2. There has always been a two-tiered early-childhood system. This is one of the fascinating points brought out by Cahan. From the beginning, we have had day nurseries (or day care or child care, to use the modern terms) for the poor, and early childhood education for the affluent. Such programs differed in their objectives and in their quality. The early day nurseries were apparently similar to the deadly institutions providing 24-hour care described by reformers of the mid-20th century. They were crowded, marginally funded, staffed by untrained personnel, and barely able to meet minimal standards of sanitation. Furthermore, as Cahan points out, they were never really "for the children." They were initially established to help the mothers. Then, during the depression, they mutated into the Works Project Administration emergency nursery schools, the primary purpose of which "was to provide work for unemployed teachers, custodians, cooks, and nurses." Serving the children was definitely of secondary concern.

Many contemporary child advocates are legitimately worried that we have no less a two-tiered system today and that not enough is being done to merge the two tracks. Even so, progress is occurring. Although many leaders of early childhood education were reluctant to form an alliance with day care, we are beginning to see evidence that most people have accepted the concept that the length of time a program operates does not specify its goal or measure its quality. Thus, it is to be hoped that by the end of this century, if not before, we can at last proclaim the eradication of one of the tracks.

3. The following formula can be derived from Cahan's text from

beginning to end: $P = f(DT, KB, SC)$, where P = Progress in early childhood, DT = Developmental Theory, KB = Knowledge Base, and SC = Social Climate. The formula says in effect that progress in early childhood has always occurred as a function of at least a triad of conditions: (a) child *development theory* stressing the importance of experiences that occur during the child's period of maximum plasticity, (b) a *knowledge base* that can offer at least a modicum of guidance about what can be accomplished through early intervention, and (c) a *social climate* receptive to applying such knowledge to existing social problems. If we were to specify the points in time at which quantum steps forward were taken in the field of early childhood, the chronicle Cahan provides us would indicate that each upward spurt in public support for early childhood programs came when all three of these conditions were present. The theory and the knowledge base have always suggested that progress is possible. However, it has consistently been economic and social needs that provided the force to move the field forward. This is just as true today as it was 200 years ago.

In view of the consistency with which these trends have operated throughout the period covered in Cahan's history, one might question just why we have made so little progress. She makes one reason abundantly clear: Early childhood programs have a long and egregious history of underfunding. Minimal standards of health care and sanitation were all that could be covered with the funds that were provided. And some of our modern child care programs are no more comfortably funded than the old day nurseries.

I would also identify at least one other factor that has slowed our progress: the resistance of the field of early childhood to pedagogical innovation and to evaluation. Most new ideas—whether involving more structure and formal teaching, computer use, or individual tutoring—are met with organized resistance, endorsement of the status quo, and even ostracism of the innovator. Likewise, until recently, evaluation of program effectiveness was anathema to many persons in the field. I have long suspected that one reason for such resistance is that many of us who ought to push the most diligently for innovation and experimentation are filled with some of the ambivalence about the effects of our services that Cahan reminds us has plagued the field from its inception. We reason that if we just stick with what is already being done, we will be obeying the Hippocratic admonition to do the least possible harm.

But the modern family has made that caution obsolete. Modern parents have clearly proclaimed their intention to rear their children collaboratively with others in the community almost from birth onward, rather than merely from age six as has been the pattern in the past. The question is no longer, Is it good for the children? but, How can it be done, and be done well?

Perhaps the best-known quote about the consequence of not knowing enough about history is George Santayana's line, which is engraved on the National Archives Building in Washington: "Those who cannot remember the past are condemned to repeat it." The collective memory in the field of childhood programs would seem to be minimal, as there is much repetition of actions that occurred in the past. Of course, we want to go on repeating some of our history. But not everything. Two hundred years is too long to have gone without strengthening our knowledge base to the point where we can point precisely to what can be expected from the different kinds of programs offered to different kinds of children for differing lengths of time with varying amounts of parent input.

Those concerned with early childhood programs should be aware of the way in which theory, knowledge, and social relevance are melded in the past and the present. They should make certain that their ideas are always tested in the crucible of real children and families. They should want to be thought of when solutions to social problems, such as welfare dependency and the prevention of delinquency, are sought. It is hoped that these aspects of the field's history, which are painstakingly chronicled for us here, will be equally visible in the future.

THE HISTORY OF PRESCHOOL CARE AND EDUCATION for children of the poor lies at the intersection of several historical questions. First, the philosophical, psychological, and educational doctrines centering on the education of the young child must be considered. Historically, pedagogical doctrines have informed the work of numerous programs and experiments in preschool education. Early education programs have also been created in the hope that they may serve as vehicles for moving individuals out of poverty, achieving greater equality among people, and realizing other forms of desired social reform.

Second, child care facilities have been created in response to patterns of maternal employment outside the home. These kinds of child care programs cannot be fully understood without considering cultural attitudes toward maternal employment and child rearing. The administration of child care programs created in response to maternal employment patterns has fallen either to the welfare system or to the federal government. When considered a function of social welfare, child care was stigmatized by the stamp of poverty. When supported by the federal government, the provision of child care was deemed a temporary emergency measure in response to national labor crises. When the crises ended, so did public support for child care.

Third, psychological (and ideological) arguments concerning the possible effects of separating young children from their caretakers (in particular, from their mothers) have often become features of debates about early childhood care and education. Objections to the separation of young children from their mothers have been raised to discourage both maternal employment and nonmaternal child care.

Finally, the history of the care and education of the poor preschool child cannot entirely be distinguished from a broader consideration of the historical treatment of the poor (and other dependent populations) in general. Because child care programs were absorbed by the welfare system, it is critical to consider broad social attitudes and policies toward the poor and dependent. In short, the questions surrounding the history of day care in general, and with particular reference to children in poverty, are complex and require a diversified response.

The interweaving of pedagogical, welfare, and reform motives in preschool programs in 18th- and 19th-century Europe and the United States was quite explicit. In particular, these programs often viewed early education as the lever for the individual reform assumed to underlie the passage from poverty to prosperity. Whether or not early education is capable of achieving true social reform without attendant changes in the structure of the economy has been much debated by historians (e.g., Lazerson, 1971) and other social critics.

Enormous variation has characterized the quality of services offered to the families of preschool children. It can be argued that such variation continues to exist. Different people invented different programs for children for different reasons, all of which held consequences both for the administration of the programs and for the type and quality of experience for the children. Much of the variation may be accounted for by economic standing. Baldly stated, poor children have tended (and still tend) to receive poor programs, while more affluent parents have always been (and remain) able to purchase higher quality programs for their children. In general, therefore, the higher quality programs remain those created for the purpose of enriching or supplementing the child's development, and the poorer quality programs tend to be those created for the purpose of providing custodial care while parents work outside the home.

Because the history of "day care" as a response to maternal employment patterns is so tightly interwoven with that of early childhood education, this monograph focuses first on the rise of a two-tier system for the care and education of the preschool child. On the one hand, for middle-income groups, there arose a nursery school and kindergarten system whose primary focus was to supplement the enrichment available at home. Diverse in their origins and purposes, nursery schools and kindergartens were held together as a system by their explicit aim of educating and socializing the growing child. On the other hand, for lower income groups, a childminding or day-care system was created in response to the necessity of maternal employment outside the home.

Second, this report will examine some of the numerous consequences for poor children and their families of such a stratified system of preschool care and education. The most important of these was the stigmatization of child care as a tool or function of social welfare—a temporary, short-term, emergency system for dealing with the "crises" surrounding maternal employment and out-of-home care for the child. Further, as a result of various "suitable home" eligibility requirements established for applicants of social welfare benefits, minorities (especially Blacks) have consistently suffered from exclusion from the system.

EARLY FORMS OF PRESCHOOL CARE AND EDUCATION

The Infant School in Europe

The charity school movement, which began in England in 1698, represents one of the earliest attempts to educate poor children by means of an organized community effort. Designed to combat various social problems perceived to be a function of the decay of religion and the rise of ignorance among the poor, the charity schools were predominantly religious in their aspirations. The movement flourished during the first half of the 18th century; by 1750, more than 30,000 children were enrolled in the schools of the Society for the Promotion of Christian Knowledge. The founders of the society wished to assist in the education of the children of the very poor "for the honor of God and the salvation of their brethren" (Forest, 1927, p. 39). Although the curriculum was predominantly religious in content, a small proportion of secular instruction was tolerated. Significantly, the education was to be arranged in such a way "that the children must still be kept contented with their 'rank and order'" in society (White & Buka, 1987, p. 39). Similar movements arose at about the same time in both the rest of Great Britain and in Europe. However none of the schools were intended for preschool children; their care and education would not become a central concern until the Industrial Revolution.

Beginning in the early 1800s, changing times and circumstances in Europe led to the creation of a number of efforts to care for and educate the preschool child. The effects of the Industrial Revolution on domestic life made it increasingly apparent that situations arose in which families were unable to provide all-day care to small children.

Reflecting on the Industrial Revolution, Florence Kelley noted that "industry affords in greater measure than the race has ever known before all those goods which form the material basis of life . . . while at the same time it disintegrates the family. This is the Paradox of Modern Industry" (Kelley, 1914, p. 1). Unable to compete with machine production, craftsmen left home to work in factories. Factory work could be done by women and children as well as or better than it could be done by men. Increases in population levels in England and the concentration of the working classes into crowded urban areas rendered the plight of the poor and oppressed visible, and "the minds and consciences of the intellectually and economically favored" were stirred "as they had never been stirred before" (Forest, 1927, p. 42). Carlton Hayes noted that "the employment of women and children seemed to have the most terrible results. The babies of factory women, weak and without proper care, died in alarming numbers . . . [W]orking women who had no homes and who were separated from their children by the factory, easily fell into immorality and vice" (Hayes, 1916, p. 81). The economist Adam Smith also noted the high mortality rate among poor children of the "common people who cannot afford to tend them with the same care as those of better station" (Smith, 1901, p.80). The effects of the Industrial Revolution seemed to be most severe on the lives of women and children.

Partly in response to these changing social conditions, programs of early education—"programs of controlled experiences for young children built upon a coherent educational philosophy" (White & Buka, 1987, p. 43) arose. Many of these programs were designed to care for the children of poor and working class parents who, because they both worked outside the home all day, were unable to provide full-time care for their children at home. These "infant schools" were created by inspired individuals who were "moved on the one hand by the impulse to help the poor child and on the other by visions of the betterment of human society" (p. 43). A brief survey of some of these infant schools will illustrate first, and perhaps most important, the longevity of our ideas concerning the plasticity and educability of the young child. Second, they demonstrate the strength of beliefs in the promise of education as a means of compensating for or rising out of poverty. A consideration of the infant school movement is relevant because of its combined concerns with educating and caring for the young, poor child whose parents worked outside the home.

Infant schools began to appear in Great Britain and Europe in the early 19th century. Some proponents felt that early education was the best means of preventing crime and juvenile delinquency. Others hoped that infant education might serve as a lever for social reform. The educator Samuel Wilderspin (1825) pleaded for infant schools as a means of protecting young children from injury. Lord Henry Brougham defended infant education "on the ground that a good deal could be done in the way of character formation at a very early age" (U.K., Lords, 1835). Brougham captured well the optimism surrounding infant education when he wrote in 1828:

> The truth is that he can and does learn a great deal more before that age [six years] than all he ever learns or can learn in all his after life. His attention is more easily aroused, his memory is more retentive, bad habits are not yet formed, nor is his judgement warped by unfair bias. (cited in Forest, 1927, p. 49)

More infant schools were established in Great Britain as families needed

"Poor children have tended (and still tend) to receive poor programs."

help and laws forbade the employment of young children. Educators agreed that the family was not always able to provide adequate education for young children and that the community must therefore join in the effort to do so. With different motives—some holy and some not so holy—the stage was set for the growth of infant schools for the poor.

In 1824 an eminent group of English reformers established an Infant School Society and solicited public subscriptions to support their innovation. Within a year, at least 55 infant schools had been established in Great Britain. Supporters embraced the idea of infant education as a means of ameliorating social problems attendant on industrial development. Seminal to the development of the infant schools was the work of two educational reformers, Johann Heinrich Pestalozzi and Robert Owen. Born in Zurich in 1747 and influenced by the writings of Jean-Jacques Rousseau, Pestalozzi founded a series of model schools in Switzerland for very young children. European and American educators often visited these famous schools. Pestalozzi hoped that by creating a homelike environment in the classroom, he would enable his teachers to add some wholesomeness to the lives of poor children. Pestalozzian teaching principles became the pedagogical core of the English infant schools.

Preschool education arrived in Scotland in 1816 when Robert Owen, founder of the British infant school movement and manager of the New Lanark Cotton Spinning Mills, opened an infant school for children whose parents worked in the mills. Owen, a utopian socialist, established the infant school as part of his model community in New Lanark. Children attended Owen's school from the age of 18 months. They were separated into age-graded groups (2-4, 4-6); at 6 or 7 the children moved into a regular classroom; and at age 10 they left school to work in the mill (Forest, 1927, 57 ff.). The school emphasized the teaching of Christian dogma and the formation of proper character. There were elements in Owen's program that we would now associate with both "day care" and early childhood education for children of working parents. In 1816, in "An Address to the Inhabitants of New Lanark," Owen defined the scope of his infant schools:

> For this purpose the Institution has been devised to afford the means of receiving your children at an early age, as soon almost as they can walk. By this means many of you, mothers of families, will be enabled to earn

a better maintenance or support for your children; you will have less care and anxiety about them; while the children will be prevented from acquiring any bad habits, and gradually prepared to learn the best. (cited in Steinfels, 1973, p. 35)

Social reformers were clearly attracted to the concept of infant schools. Children would benefit from both early character training and an education in Christian dogma while their mothers and older siblings were free to work in the mills.

Two schools modeled on Owen's were established in London—one by Lord Brougham together with James Mill and one by the Society of Friends with Samuel Wilderspin as director. Wilderspin's infant school was more highly structured than its predecessor in New Lanark and more fully aligned with the instructional goals of elementary schooling. Though Wilderspin, unlike Owen, was not interested in using the infant school as a building block for a better society, his influence—through lectures, the eight reprintings of his 1840 book, The *Infant System of Developing the Intellectual and Moral Powers of all Children from One to Seven*, and promotional efforts—led to the opening of about 150 infant schools in a period of 10 years (Whitbread, 1972, pp. 12–14). Wilderspin hoped that infant schools would help prevent crime and delinquency and, at the same time, reform parents.

A French Lutheran pastor, Jean Frédéric Oberlin, struck by the poverty and degradation of children in rural areas of the Vosges, opened at his own expense *écoles à tricoter* (knitting schools). Oberlin attempted to teach young children morality, good habits, and scriptural stories. He prepared children for school and taught older children to sew and knit. Like Owen, Oberlin sought moral redemption and social reform through the education of the young child. Other public-spirited people in France opened *salles d'asile* (places of refuge) for working-class children in the early 1800s. A Mme. Pastoret, having heard of Oberlin's work, opened a *salle de l'hospitalité* to protect little children from the dangers of the city streets in France. By 1838 there were 19 such refuges in Paris, serving 3,600 children. Enactments in 1837 and 1838 brought the management of the infant schools under the French educational system.

In Belgium *écoles-gardiennes* opened to provide care and education for children whose mothers worked outside the home. In Belgium too, as in France and England, infant schools gained some recognition and support from the government. The reasons for and hopes surrounding these infant schools varied. The apparent "neglect of little children whose parents' resources were limited" seems to have been the driving motive behind most

A crèche day nursery in Buffalo, New York, 1885. This type of facility spread rapidly through the urban East in the 1880s.

Culver

of them (Forest, 1927, p. 68). J.D.M. Cochin explained that many children were deprived of their mothers' care "not only by inevitable death, but because of the necessities of labor" (Cochin, 1853, p. 16). Similarly, in Germany, *Kleinkinderbewahranstalten* (schools of necessity) existed primarily to "take care of children whose mothers were obliged to work" (Forest, 1927, p. 72).

In Italy, an abbot, Ferrante Aporti, opened an infant school in Cremona in 1828 because he was dissatisfied with children's progress in elementary schools. In the same year, Maria Montessori extended her work with retarded children to working with children from the slums of Rome. In 1833, Aporti published his *Manual of Education and Teaching for Infant Schools*, stressing the importance of moral habits, intellectual stimulation, and physical activity.

Controversy surrounded infant schools, however. Some critics feared that if poor children were educated they would become discontented with their lot in life. Other critics felt that separating young children from their mothers for prolonged periods of time violated the laws of God and nature (Forest, 1927, p. 79).

This brief survey of the early infant school movement in Europe illuminates the varied motives and foundations for the care and education of the preschool child. The programmatic responses to the problems surrounding the new industrial order included providing for both the care and the education of the preschool child. Many infant schools eventually gained some lasting measure of state support in several countries. Perhaps most crucial, the existence of these infant schools clarifies the staying power of our ideas about the importance of early experience in laying the foundation for later development. It also illustrates the role of education as a means of overcoming poverty and its accompanying social problems.

Infant Schools in the United States

The 19th century saw the establishment first of infant schools and, later, of kindergartens—both created to shift some of the traditional family responsibilities of early childhood to the schools. In both periods, according to Tank (1980), two now-familiar arguments supporting early education were advanced by two loosely knit groups of people, each with different motives. One group promoted early education with the argument that lower income families were incapable of properly socializing their children. Tank (1980) refers to these efforts as the first American attempt to establish "poverty track educational institutions as practical alternatives to the traditional family-centered socialization process" (p. 16).

The second group based its support for early education on the potential benefits that would accrue to young children from a program attuned to their developmental needs—one that also prepared them for elementary school. In the 1820s and 1830s, these people promoted infant education as a kind of "head start" for children's educational careers. At the turn of the century, they supported kindergartens that promised to enrich the experiences of all children. In reality, however, these "child-centered" enrichment programs were limited to the middle and upper economic strata of American society. Thus, we may be able to trace the origins of the two-tier system of early child care and education in this country by examining the history and fate of the short-lived infant school movement in the United States.

Following the lead of the European infant school movement, American educators and social reformers were also attracted to the idea of using early education as a means to teach morality to the children of poverty. From his base in Boston as a publisher and educator, Scottish-born William Russell led the American effort to teach young poor children "moral habits." Russell insisted that these "poverty track" infant schools could be effective levers of moral reform. By the late 1820s, civic-minded social elites in New York, Philadelphia, and Boston had opened infant schools with moralistic intentions.

Formed by a group of evangelical women interested in providing religious instruction, preschool education, and day care for young children of the urban poor, the Infant School Society of Boston was founded in 1828. Trustees of the Boston Infant School justified their intent by indicating that "such a school would be of eminent service, both to parents and to children. By relieving mothers of a part of their domestic cares, it would enable them to seek employment." At the same time, the children "would be removed from the unhappy association of want and vice, and be placed under better influences. . . ." (Infant School Society of Boston, 1828). Children would be accepted between the ages of 18 months and 4 years. The school would be open from 6 A.M. to 7 P.M. in the summer and from 8 A.M. to 5 P.M. in the winter. Although detailed information on the number and extent of the Boston Infant Schools is not readily available, one author estimates that the Infant School Society may have operated as many as five infant schools at different locations in and around Boston between the years 1828 and 1835, when the movement dissipated. A sliding tuition scale of 2¢ a day allowed children to attend regardless of parental income. The society was supported, in descending order of magnitude, by private donations, fund-raising, annual dues of member schools, and tuition (Beatty, 1981).

In addition to religious instruction and moral training, the schools instructed children in Pestalozzian object lessons and offered brief didactic periods, movement and exercise, story reading, outdoor play, marching, clapping, and sewing two afternoons a week as "a reward for good behavior" (cited in Beatty, 1981, p. 27).

The women of the Infant School Society viewed their work as an extension of that of their husbands for the Society for the Religious and Moral Instruction of the Poor. While the men were responsible for the religious education of the school-age youngster, the women in the Infant School Society worked with preschool children. Both groups were centrally concerned with morally reforming the poor. The *Sixth Annual Report* of the Boston Infant School Society warned that "the seeds of folly" which were "bound up in the heart of a child, may spring to a prematurity in . . . hotbeds of vice, and before they are four years old . . . bring forth bitter fruits" (cited in Beatty, 1981, p. 23).

For early 19th century Americans, poverty was a spiritual problem, not an economic problem. And "the bitterness of poverty" consisted "not so much in its privations as in its temptations" (cited in Beatty, 1981, p. 24).

> *"In the early 1830s . . . the child's
> home was deemed the most appropriate
> environment for early development, and the
> informed mother was deemed the best teacher."*

The hope was to eradicate poverty with aid from the Infant Schools in three generations.

In addition, however, to providing "antidotes" to the effects of lower-class child-rearing practices, infant schools provided care for children whose parents worked outside the home and promised to work as agents of parental reform. One supporter asserted that infant schools would "greatly relieve the parents from the waste of time and anxiety attendant on the care of their children—it will thus increase their capacity to earn subsistence" (cited in Kuhn, 1947). Advocates further hoped that the lessons learned by the children in the infant schools would pervade the home and, in doing so, the adult poor would be instructed in the mores of society. A mixture of anxiety and compassion is illustrated in an article in a Boston magazine:

> Will you not remember . . . those poor little ones who have no nursery and no mother deserving the name? And will you not . . . come forward and afford your aid to their cause, and not rest till every section of the city has its Infant School? (cited in Kuhn, 1947, p. 27)

Increasing attention began to be focused on the special knowledge and understanding of children that women were presumed to bring to the task of educating the young child. Women were thought to know better than men "how much may be done towards forming the mental and especially the moral character, during the first four years of a child's life" (cited in Kuhn, 1947, p. 27).

Infant education in the United States was not restricted to efforts to reform the urban poor. Affluent parents in such cities as New York, Hartford, Cincinnati, Detroit, and numerous rural communities surrounding Boston sent their children to infant schools in order to give them a kind of "head start" in their schooling. An article in the *Ladies Magazine* alluded to the possible benefits of infant education for upper class children:

> And why should a plan which promises so many advantages, independent of merely relieving the mother from her charge, be confined to the children of the indigent? It is nearly if not quite impossible, to teach such little ones

at home with the facility they are taught in an infant school. And if a convenient room is prepared, and faithful and discreet agents employed, parents may feel secure that their darlings are not only safe, but improving. (Anon., 1829, p. 89)

In Boston, too, the infant education movement extended to more affluent families seeking to provide their children with the same educational opportunities they believed were being offered to poor children. These higher income families sent their children to private infant schools where the emphasis was exclusively on early enrichment and not on moral reform of either the parents or their children. However, these infant schools for the children of the affluent probably remained few in number compared to the infant schools established for the children of the poor (Beatty, 1981).

In New York City, an infant school for the affluent captured the imagination of reformers who, in the interests of preserving the social order against unrest, founded an Infant School Society. These infant schools enrolled young children of "indigent and uneducated parents" who were unable to provide that "personal and moral culture" traditionally imparted to children by their parents. As in New York, groups of reformers in Philadelphia established infant schools to guide the moral, spiritual, and character development of young poor children and to help prepare them for public schools.

The infant school movement in the United States was short-lived. Interest in infant schools ceased in New York in 1832 when the Public School Society established primary schools. Similar events occurred in different cities. The Boston Primary School Board rejected the idea of incorporating infant schools into the public system of primary education on economic grounds. Some felt that the program of moral reformation characterizing the infant schools in Boston was inconsistent with the emphasis on teaching reading and spelling through discipline and rote memory. Other teachers reported that graduates of the infant schools were "less teachable" than their untutored peers (Beatty, 1981).

The rising tide of a domestic ethic also contributed to the demise of the infant school movement. In the early 1830s and thereafter, the child's home was deemed the most appropriate environment for early development, and the informed mother was deemed the best teacher. This strong revival, dating back to colonial times, of the notion that the young child should be educated at home, eroded support for the infant school movement. An article in the *American Journal of Education* enumerated some of the arguments against infant schools:

It is objected to them that they furnish occasion for remissness in the discharge of parental duties, by devolving the care of infancy on teachers, instead of leaving with the mother the full weight and responsibility of her natural relation. The strength of domestic attachment in the child is also said to be weakened, by removing him for a considerable part of the day from home, and furnishing him with enjoyments of a higher kind than he could experience there. (cited in Beatty, 1981, p. 29)

Finally, an influential book by Amariah Brigham, *Remarks on the Influence of Mental Excitement upon Health* (1833), argued that schooling might in fact harm young children. Brigham claimed that early schooling might cause physical illness or even insanity and that young children needed more physical exercise and less mental cultivation. Donations to the infant schools from upper class supporters fell off sharply. The hostility toward early childhood education generated by Brigham's book through its influence on the domestic literature might well have "sounded the death knell of the infant school movement" (Tank, 1980, p. 31).

Tank (1980) concludes his analysis of the infant education movement in the United States by suggesting that these contrasting motives for early childhood intervention persisted and formed the basis for two very different cultural inventions in the latter half of the 19th century and the beginning decades of the 20th century—the day nursery for children of poor parents and the nursery school for children of more affluent parents. Throughout the rest of this period, the primacy of the family as the ideal agent of childhood socialization and early learning would go unchallenged. With the passing away of infant schools, the care of preschool children whose parents worked fell to the day nurseries, and the early education of the middle-class preschooler fell to the private nursery school and kindergarten. In the years to come, nursery schools, kindergartens, and day nurseries would become increasingly differentiated from one another.

The Day Nursery

The following sections detail some of the early history of the day nursery and nursery school movements. Together, these movements consolidated a two-tier system for the care and education of the preschool child.

The concept of a day nursery to care exclusively for children whose parents were away from home at work originated in France with the invention of the crèche. The first crèche had opened in 1844 in Chaillot, on the outskirts of Paris, as part of an effort to combat infant mortality. So great

> *"Throughout the 19th and into the 20th century . . . work, rather than alms, was held to be the desired solution to the problems of the poor."*

was the demand for low-paid, unskilled factory workers that many industrial firms sponsored crèches so that mothers could breast-feed their babies and continue their work in the mills (Beer, 1957, pp. 27–30; Forest, 1927, pp. 310–311).

In the last quarter of the 19th century, a growing child study and child welfare movement brought attention to the plight of poor children in a rapidly industrializing and increasingly urban America. In 1875 the National Conference on Charities and Corrections included, for the first time, child welfare on its agenda. As the 19th century came to a close, the plight of poor children in America attracted an increasing amount of attention from charity workers. Some of the many new expressions of this concern for "child saving" included the establishment of Sunday school classes, missions, orphan homes, children's aid societies, settlement houses, kindergarten education, tenement house and child labor reform; campaigns to conserve the health of infants and young children; campaigns to remove young paupers from the almshouses; the establishment of reformatories and probationary measures for young offenders; programs to send orphaned children out West to live with farm families; and mothers' pensions as an economic aid to single-parent families (Brace, 1872/1973; Siegel & White, 1982). An increasing number of people involved in child-saving activities perceived poor children as the most innocent victims of poverty. The plight of poor children was more distressing than adult poverty because children were "no more responsible for their poverty than they were for their birth" (Bremner, 1956, pp. 212–213).

As concern for the children of poverty rose in the last quarter of the 19th century, some social reformers and charity workers turned their attention to the plight of poor children in need of child care—the "large number of neglected children who must be either left to the tender mercies of the neighbor or be cared for by some small substitute mother"—while their mothers worked. They turned to the day nursery, in part, "to safeguard the well-being of unsupervised toddlers" (Rosenau, 1894, p. 334).

Between the years 1878 and 1916, the number of day nurseries in the United States grew from 3 to approximately 700. Day nurseries were one of many efforts to help children by keeping families intact. Consistent with the wishes of organized charity workers, day nurseries were designed "to keep the family together if it is within the bounds of reason to do so" (National Conference, 1902, p. 179). The original purpose of the National Federation of Day Nurseries, established in 1898, was that of "assisting the broken family by offering day shelter for the children" (Lewinsky-Corwin, 1923, n.p.).

The day nursery was also one expression of a wider movement to get poor children out of institutions and back into the homes of their families. The 19th century witnessed both the building and the partial dismantling of institutional care as an acceptable means of dealing with poor children. James Brown characterized this history succinctly when he wrote: "We can sum up the history of child welfare in the nineteenth century by saying that the first half was devoted to getting dependent children into the almshouses and the second half to getting them out" (Brown, 1960, p. 196). The day nursery and, later, mothers' pensions were both conceived of as measures to prevent the institutionalization of poor children. Preventing such institutionalization was a motive for establishing day nurseries that cut across color lines. In describing the Hope Day Nursery for Black children in New York, Griffin (1906) commented that "working mothers are beginning to realize that with the day nursery their homes are kept together, and the need for placing children in institutions for a term of years is lessened" (p. 400).

Insofar as day nurseries were conceived of as a form of social welfare, their history is more closely tied in this period to that of the welfare system than it is to the history of early childhood education. The following pages detail some of the consequences of child care falling into the embryonic social welfare system. One must remember too that this young American social welfare system was largely a system designed by and created for the benefit of whites. Although no adequate history of Black voluntarism exists at this time, it is known that "the virtual absence of social welfare institutions in many Southern communities and the frequent exclusion of Blacks from those that existed, led Black women to found orphanages, old folks' homes and similar institutions," including kindergartens and day nurseries (Lerner, 1974, p. 159).

Early Growth of Day Nurseries

Evidence suggests that families with working mothers in this period relied on a variety of child care arrangements. Some mothers—especially those employed in domestic service—took their children with them to work; some left their children in the care of their husbands, older children, relatives, neighbors, or friends. Some mothers, inevitably, were forced to leave their children unattended at home. Many of these arrangements were haphazard at best and, at worst, downright dangerous for the children. The available nurseries were overcrowded and often located in surroundings unsuitable for young children:

> One woman occupying four dark, poorly ventilated rooms was crowding into them thirty or forty children each day; another was caring for twelve children in equally bad surroundings; a third, with less than one-tenth vision, was receiving fourteen children in her two rooms; and a fourth was caring for eight children whom she was in the habit of shutting behind two locked doors on the second floor while she did her marketing. (Anon., 1918, p. 229)

Clearly, many mothers were desperate in their search for child care. As one social worker noted, it was the "resourceless mother, the poverty-stricken wife or widow, or the deserted woman without relatives or friends, who was compelled by circumstances to make unfavorable child care arrangements" (Tyson, 1924, p. 12). More often than not, these "resourceless" mothers were European immigrants or other recent arrivals forced to make their way into the labor market.

Beginning around the middle of the 19th century, groups of philanthropically inclined women began to establish day nurseries for those working mothers who were unable to make satisfactory informal arrangements. These day nurseries were explicit responses to the problems surrounding the competing demands of maternal employment and child care for the children of poor, working parents.

The first American crèche was opened in 1854 in New York by Nurse's and Children's Hospital "for the maintenance and care of children of wet nurses, and the care of infants whose parents labored away from home" (Nursery for the Children, 1854, p. 1). For a fee of 5¢ a day, this "Nursery for the Children of Poor Women" tended to the physical needs of children ranging in age from 6 weeks to 6 years. A first priority of the nursery was to maintain the children's cleanliness and personal hygiene.

Four years later, a group of charitable women in Troy, New York, opened a day nursery modeled after that at Nurse's and Children's Hospital. The only other American day nursery before 1879 was founded in Philadelphia during the Civil War. The founder, a "Miss Biddle," had traveled to Paris and observed a crèche serving young children of mothers who worked in local hospitals and factories, and she consciously modeled her Philadelphia day nursery along Parisian lines. At home in the United States, Miss

> " *'Children of wage-earning mothers absent all day from home, exhausted by hard labor, and pitiably recompensed' were no better off than the 'full orphan.' "*

Biddle, a charitably inclined spinster, was "touched by the condition of the little ones of absent working mothers whom she often found locked alone in their rooms" (Babcock, 1904). Miss Biddle's group child care center in Philadelphia subsequently served as a model for other poverty-track day nurseries.

Led by developments in New York, Boston, Philadelphia, and Cleveland, day nurseries spread rapidly throughout the urban Northeast in the 1880s and 1890s. By 1892 religious and charitable organizations had opened approximately 90 day nurseries to care for the children of working mothers. In 1898 the 175 day nurseries operating throughout the country consolidated into the National Federation of Day Nurseries. The federation strove to "unite in one central body all day nurseries and to endeavor to secure the highest attainable standards of merit" (White House Conference, 1931, p. 15). However, the demand for day nursery services would always outstrip the supply.

Quality and Range of Services in Day Nurseries

Day nurseries varied widely with respect to both the quality and quantity of available services. Early day nurseries, however, tended to define their tasks rather narrowly. For the most part, they provided "day nursery children with a simple, quiet, clean day home" (M. Dewey, 1897, p. 105). Again and again, as one reads descriptions of these early day nurseries, one is forced to conclude that they were almost always limited to providing only minimal forms of care and protection for the children.

Day nurseries were typically located in converted houses, brownstones, or unused stores. Available evidence suggests that the children engaged in few organized games and activities. Occasionally, a side yard or a rooftop served as a playground for exercise and play. The first priority for most nurseries was to maintain cleanliness. While most day nurseries expected their charges to arrive at the nursery clean, many children arrived unwashed. The better day nurseries took some pride in their efforts to bathe and provide each child with a set of clean nursery clothes. The child's own clothes would then be aired and disinfected. Such was the hygienic ideal, but few day nurseries had the facilities or the personnel to undertake these tasks.

In *Working Mothers and the Day Nursery*, Ethel Beer recalls the early days of the nursery school:

> My first impression of Brightside Day Nursery was anything but favorable. The building was gloomy.... and row after row of ugly iron cribs with plaques advertising their donors left little space to play on this floor or the one above used by the younger preschool group. . . . On the whole, the personnel was untrained and some were mentally dull. The diet was sadly lacking in vitamins. Orange juice and cod-liver oil were considered too extravagant to provide. Even milk was a scarce commodity. (Beer, 1957, pp. 43–44)

In their desire to serve families, some day nurseries offered a kind of employment service to help mothers find employment. The Leila Day Nursery in New Haven, for example, operated an "intelligence department" that placed widows and wives of drunkards in middle- and upper-class homes as laundresses and domestics (Tank, 1980, p. 123). In a similar effort, New York City`s West Side Day Nursery placed mothers as washerwomen and cleaners in homes and as kitchen help in local restaurants.

These efforts to aid mothers in the search for employment illustrate also a more general preference on the part of social welfare workers for self-help through work rather than charity. Supporters of the day nursery hoped that the nurseries would enable parents of young children to support and maintain their families through work. Throughout the 19th and into the 20th century, philanthropists believed that outdoor relief encouraged the poor to remain dependent. Work, rather than alms, was held to be the desired solution to the problems of the poor. In 1877 the New York Charity Organization's fifth annual report stated that "honest employment . . . the work that God means every man to do is the truest basis of relief for every person with physical ability to work" (cited in Lubove, 1965, p. 8). The day nursery appealed to the charity worker's disdain for outdoor relief while affirming the value of work and self-help. The Leila Day Nursery of New Haven pledged to "help those who helped themselves" (Conference of Day Nurseries, 1892, p. 16). Similarly, the day nursery association in Cleveland adopted the precept that "only through work could day nursery parents help themselves" (cited in Tank, 1980, p. 123).

Few day nurseries were able to provide three quality meals a day to the children. With limited resources, they did the best they could to provide the children with nourishing meals and snacks. In many cases, however, the diet provided was "inadequate" and the food of "inferior grade." At the Brightside Day Nursery, watery vegetable soup and thin cocoa were prominent menu items, and "only the weak children were given milk regularly. And they had to have a doctor's prescription for it" (Beer, 1957, p. 44). Beer's account emphasizes that the situation at Brightside was "no exception." The details at other day nurseries might vary, but "on the whole the atmosphere was the same" (Beer, 1957, p. 44).

Early day nurseries in the United States remained largely custodial institutions for the simple reason that they lacked sufficient resources to be anything more elaborate. It was not uncommon for one matron to be responsible for cooking, cleaning, laundering, and supervising between 30 and 50 preschool children. She "must do all the housekeeping, make all the purchases of supplies, attend to the linen, and see to the cooking" as well as "a thousand and one things which a mother is called upon to do" (Rosenau, 1894, p 336). The St. Agnes Day Nursery in New York City simply instructed its matron "to prepare and give the children their meals, to keep them clean, and to take general charge of them" (St. Agnes Day Nursery, 1888, pp. 5–6).

Day Nurseries and Blacks

Thus far this account has surveyed a movement that was predominantly white. Clearly, most day nursery activity did occur among whites in the urban Northeast. However, increasing evidence suggests that by the 1890s a parallel but independent movement to establish child care facilities existed among Blacks (Billingsley & Giovannoni, 1972; Cunningham & Osborn, 1979). By the 1890s, Black women trained in churches and in secret orders, prepared to take up "club work," and in 1893, Black women's clubs were operating in Washington, Philadelphia, New York, Boston, Chicago, St. Louis, Kansas City, Topeka, and elsewhere (Yates, 1905). Part of the club work—among both whites and Blacks—concerned child welfare. In 1902 the National Council of Women made the following pledge to help the National Association of Colored Women (established in 1896) in any way possible, but with particular attention to its day nurseries and kindergarten work:

> Resolved, That the National Council of Women, in order that the progress of the colored people of the United States along all lines of human endeavor may become better known, shall keep before the public in every way possible, the facts presented on the subject; and assist in founding and maintaining kindergartens and day nurseries, especially among the poorer classes of colored people. (cited in Yates, 1905, p. 308)

Alvin Maurice Cahan, M.D.

**The nursery school of the Child Development Institute at Teachers College,
Columbia University, New York City, 1930.**

The creation of day nurseries for Black children resulted from the prevailing race prejudice of the times. In New York City, Black "mothers seeking admittance for their babies at the nurseries already established, found that they were either too crowded or opposed to accommodating Negroes" (Griffin, 1906, p. 397). The few nurseries in New York that did accept Blacks would only accept two or three at a time. In May 1903, in New York, a committee of Black women opened the first day nursery for Black children, the Hope Day Nursery.

A commentator remarked that the Hope Day Nursery was

> the only institution of the kind maintained principally for colored mothers whose various work takes them from home all day, with the alternative of leaving their children alone or in charge of different caretakers who, as a rule, are more mindful of the remuneration than of the infants for whose keeping it is received. (Griffin, 1906, p. 397)

Expanding Services

Also around the turn of the century, in spite of meager resources, some day nurseries tried to address the child's educational, developmental, socialization, and health needs—elements of what today we associate with quality child care. A few nurseries, including the Hope Day Nursery, tried to offer a modest educational program based on the work of the traditional kindergarten. Faith that "the greatest possibilities for helping the poor [lay] in the care and training of children" attracted charity workers to the kindergarten (Anon., 1902, p. 543). "As kindergarten training has appealed to the public's intelligence," wrote the president of the National Federation of Day Nurseries in 1897, "it has been included in the nursery regime" (Dodge, 1897, p. 62). In Cleveland, for example, the local day nursery association operated a kindergarten in each of its five nurseries, enrolled a total of 586 children in 1914, and declared its belief that without an educational component the work of the nursery was incomplete (Dodge, 1897). In Chicago, the beneficence of a philanthropically minded local woman made possible the establishment of a combined day nursery and kindergarten program for the children of working mothers.

Elsewhere, heartened by success, kindergarten and day nursery association workers expanded their work with children to include social and educational services for adults. In these ways, many day nurseries became akin to full-fledged settlement houses. Following the lead set by settlements in Detroit and Boston, by 1905 several settlement houses in other cities were operating both a day nursery and a kindergarten under one roof. Children from the nursery would attend kindergarten classes for part of the day. Clearly, many settlement workers recognized early childhood education as an important component of child care.

Like the kindergarten itself, day nurseries after 1900 increasingly sought to socialize and help immigrant children and their parents assimilate themselves to American society. In describing the Hull House Day Nursery, Jane Addams indicated that it was a place where immigrant children "are taught the things which will make life in America more possible" (Addams, 1910, p. 169). Lessons ranged from manners and eating habits to proper moral dispositions.

Other innovations in the day nursery in the period before World War I included a program of after-school care for older children. Distressed workers at the Fitch Crèche in Buffalo found "that a good many of the children who had been graduated from the Crèche were running about the streets after school hours" (Rosenau, 1894, p. 339). Some nurseries also provided emergency night care and child care for working mothers who became ill and therefore could not care for their children.

In the early years of the 20th century, many day nurseries tried to promote child health. A few generously sponsored nurseries, such as the

---

> *"Except in unusual circumstances, the home*
> *should not be broken up for reasons*
> *of poverty, but only for considerations of*
> *inefficiency or immorality."*

Fitch Crèche in Buffalo, employed a full-time nurse to supervise health care. Some nurseries, such as New York City's Brightside Day Nursery and those run by the Cleveland Day Nursery and Free Kindergarten Association included daily examinations for the children from a physician (Cleveland Day Nursery, 1892, p. 9). More commonly, children received a brief physical examination on entrance to the day nursery to ensure against contagion.

Still other innovative efforts reflected the growing parent education movement among middle-class parents. "Mothers' clubs" formed around some nurseries in order to hold weekly or biweekly evening classes in sewing, cooking, and child care. Some nurseries held health care and hygiene classes for mothers. Day nursery workers agreed that ignorance among mothers was a serious problem, finding that "nurseries have within them the possibilities for serving as centers of information regarding the health care of young children" (cited in Tank, 1980, p. 140). It is important to note, however, that before World War I the vast majority of day nurseries were unable to provide such innovative services. These innovations attest to the efforts of some day nursery workers to broaden the range of services available beyond custodial care and to respond to the variety of issues surrounding poor children and families.

The Day Nursery under Fire

After 1900 the day nursery fell into increasing disrepute. Critics of group child care became both more numerous and more outspoken. Jane Addams, herself an innovator in the day nursery movement, outlined an argument against group child care. For 16 years, she sponsored a day nursery at the Hull House settlement to care for children whose mothers were "bent under the double burden of earning the money which supports them and giving their children the tender care which alone keeps them alive" (Addams, 1910, p. 169). However, daily encounters with mothers who were both "father and mother to their children" led Addams to become disillusioned, question the legitimacy of the day nursery, and wonder if it should "tempt" mothers to "attempt the impossible."

Robert Woods, the leading settlement worker in Boston, also came to doubt the worth of the day nursery. Settlement workers in Boston began to feel that "children of wage-earning mothers absent all day from home, exhausted by hard labor, and pitiably recompensed" were no better off than the "full orphan" (Woods & Kennedy, 1922, p. 195). In 1910, the Tyler Street Day Nursery in Boston closed not for lack of funds but "because its promoters became convinced that it was doing more harm than good" (Hartt, 1911, p. 22). The North Bennett Street Nursery limited admissions to "cases" in which the "expert" friendly visitors were satisfied that the nursery was an "adequate answer to the family problem of the poor" (p. 22). Critics insisted that the day nursery contributed to the decline of family life. The following case illustrates dramatically many of the problems relating to the poor and the day nursery in the early years of this century:

> Take our star case, an Italian widow with three children. Till the father died they had never needed help. The mother got work in a chocolate factory dipping candies six days in the week from eight to five, earning a maximum wage of five dollars. Relatives helped a little and the Associated Charities "chipped in" to the extent of a dollar and a half a week. The day nursery took the two younger children and fed the older boy his dinner after school until he got too big to have it among little tots.

> The mother has worked miracles. The four have lived, bathed, slept, cooked and eaten, in a single room. Yet there has never been the ghost of a 'poor' smell. Her floor is clean enough to eat off. She has fed and clothed her children economically and intelligently. She has maintained their self-respect. But to do it she has spent half her nights in washing, ironing, scrubbing, or mending. Three years of superhuman effort on her part, and a weekly expenditure of five dollars for the care of her children. Result, what? Overwork is slowly killing the mother, while for the lack of her control by day the older boy is getting into juvenile court! And that is our star case. (Hartt, 1911, pp. 22–23)

Settlement workers, day nursery workers, and charity workers alike weighed the benefits of day nursery care against the costs to families when mothers attempted to fill the triple role of breadwinner, child rearer, and homemaker. Critics claimed that "the home crumbles" and the "physical and moral well-being of the mother and the children is seriously menaced" under the burdens of multiple roles (Anon., 1914, p. 809). Grace Abbott, who began her distinguished career as a settlement worker and eventually became director of the Children's Bureau, commented that even the most coura-geous and hard-working mother "broke down under the double burden of wage-earner and housekeeper, and the children were first neglected and then delinquent" (Abbott, 1938, p. 230). With prescience, Abbott contended that day nurseries were not a necessary part of child welfare services and that the nation could well afford to support mothers at home.

Finally, a new generation of professional philanthropists did not entirely trust the women who often composed the boards of day nurseries. Some philanthropists accused charity workers of carelessness and indiscriminate generosity toward clients. Edward Devine politely expressed his reservations about such indiscriminate relief:

> It has already become reasonably clear that indiscriminate aid in the form of care for children in day nurseries is nearly as objectionable as any other indiscriminate relief. To enable the mother to work when the father is lazy or shiftless or incompetent is sometimes to incur direct responsibility for perpetuating bad family conditions . . . Such are the economic and social problems which are beginning to complicate the day nursery, as indeed, they affect all charitable work. They are not incapable of solution. Here, as in other forms of child-saving work a snare lies before those who hope "to save the child," disregarding the other members of the family. The family must be considered as a whole. Neither the child nor the adult can be dealt with separately. The managers of the day nursery who are actuated by a desire to be of real service to the families whose children are received must in each instance face the question as to whether the family is a proper one to receive this particular form of assistance—whether the result in this particular instance is likely on the whole to be beneficial. (Devine, 1910, pp. 339–340)

In these and other ways, questions of propriety, appropriateness, or "worthiness" began to play a dominant role in the administration of day nursery services.

The Beginnings of Social Casework in the Day Nursery

As the 19th century drew to a close, traditional American fears about and ambivalence toward both charity and maternal employment combined in a way that forced day nurseries to differentiate the "worthy" from the "unworthy" poor. Some charity workers feared that helping mothers gain employment would encourage "a lazy father in his indolence"—that by relieving fathers of their proper social responsibilities day nurseries were "fostering the charity habit" (cited in Tank, 1980, p. 125). Thus, only the children of "worthy," deserving parents should be cared for by the day nursery because:

> *"The newly professionalized social workers*
> *reinforced the growing stigmatization of*
> *out-of-home child care for children*
> *of working poor parents."*

to care for and nourish the children of unworthy parents (while at the same time allowing their parents to keep possession of their children and continue in their own evil ways) is to encourage such unworthiness in others who are only kept from the fall by fear of the consequences (M. Dewey, 1897, p. 105).

Therefore, as early as the 1890s, some day nurseries began to screen applicants to ensure that nursery services were encouraging neither the purchase of luxury items nor paternal irresponsibility. This rise of "friendly visiting" to investigate clients marked the beginning of a trend toward reliance on casework methods being developed in the then-emerging social work profession.

During the early years of the day nursery movement, the ideal of family preservation served as a source of sanction and support. Most charity workers at the time believed that the nursery was a benign substitute for home and mother. By 1910, however, this same commitment to home and family began to work against the day nursery movement. Increasingly, charity workers and, in particular, the new social workers trained in casework methods believed that the home was the only proper place for children and that the mother was the best caretaker. Again, Jane Addams argued:

> With all the efforts made by modern society to nurture and educate the young, how stupid it is to permit the mothers of young children to spend themselves in the coarser work of the world! It is curiously inconsistent with the emphasis which this generation has placed upon the mother and upon the prolongation of infancy, that we constantly allow the waste of this most precious material. (Addams, 1910, p. 174)

Thus, with its joint emphasis on assistance to the poor and the management of services by charity workers, the day nursery assumed a place in the embryonic U.S. social welfare system. Ambivalence about the poor and about maternal employment shaped the attitudes of many toward the day nursery—which was itself seen to represent a consequence of both poverty and maternal employment. A second layer of ambivalence toward the day nursery was fueled by the strengthening domestic ethic—an ethic that propounded self-reliance in families and the centrality of parents (especially mothers) to the child-rearing process. Social workers predicted that "the need for the day nursery would decline in proportion to the increasing capabilities of families, especially of newcomers, to discharge the normal socialization process of child rearing" (M. Dewey, 1897, p. 105). The function of the day nursery was therefore to hasten the arrival of the day when its services would no longer be needed. Conceiving of the day nursery as a temporary aid to troubled families enabled child care supporters to reconcile their beliefs about the importance of home rearing of children with the social welfare emphasis on work and self-help. The day nursery thus existed "under sufferance" in these years and did not signal any sort of shift in attitudes toward either the poor or children.

The Movement for Mothers' Pensions

In 1909, President Theodore Roosevelt opened the White House Conference on the Care of Dependent Children by declaring that dependent mothers should raise their own children:

> In cases where the father has died, where the breadwinner has gone, where the mother would like to keep the child, but simply lacks the earning capacity . . . the goal toward which we should strive is to help that mother so that she can keep her own home and keep the child in it; that is the best thing possible to be done for that child. (*Proceedings*, 1909, p. 36)

Speakers at the conference agreed that the role of the mother was to provide for the moral, mental, and physical education of her children, and that "the mother is not expected to become the breadwinner" (*Proceedings*, 1909, p. 36). Finally, Roosevelt concluded the conference with his famous declaration of the values of home life and motherhood:

> Home life is the highest and finest product of civilization. It is the great molding force of mind and of character. Children should not be deprived of it except for urgent or compelling reasons. Children of parents of worthy character, suffering from temporary misfortune, and children of reasonably efficient and deserving mothers who are without the support of the normal breadwinner, should as a rule be kept with their parents, such aid being given as may be necessary to maintain suitable homes for the rearing of the children . . . Except in unusual circumstances, the home should not be broken up for reasons of poverty, but only for considerations of inefficiency or immorality. (pp. 17–18)

By 1911 it was clear that the day nursery was at best "makeshift," a "necessary evil," and at worst a partner of an industrial system "trying its evil best to thrust the working man's wife or widow, the mother of the working man's children, out of her home and into its insatiable mills" (Hartt, 1911, p. 24). Alternative ways of supporting poor mothers with young children were to be sought that would preserve the mother's traditional role as primary caretaker of her children—a role that was increasingly seen as being threatened by the day nursery. A social innovation invented as a measure to rescue families now faced its demise because it was perceived as threatening to the very structure it was created to support. Thus were mothers' pensions ushered into the new welfare state in America.

Critics of day nurseries were prominent supporters of the new movement to provide mothers' pensions. Pensions to mothers with dependent children represented a form of public assistance that enabled children to be cared for in the home rather than in day nurseries, orphan asylums, or foster homes (Leff, 1973). Historically, the pensions program was the direct predecessor of Aid to Dependent Children (ADC), which was founded as part of the Social Security Administration in 1935 and became Aid to Families with Dependent Children (AFDC) in 1962 (Bell, 1965).

Between 1911 and 1915, 29 states, and by 1919, 39 states plus Alaska and Hawaii, passed mothers' pension legislation. Often accompanied by statutes regulating child labor, working conditions, minimum wages for women and children, and tenement reform, mothers' pensions were a popular measure that epitomized many of the progressive social reform impulses of the time. According to Abbott (1938), enactment of mothers' pension legislation constituted public recognition that "the contribution of the unskilled or semiskilled mother in her own home exceeded her earnings outside the home and that it was in the public interest to conserve her child caring function" (p. 229). Proponents of mothers' pensions considered them not as a charity dole but rather as a payment to mothers for the service of caring for their children.

At the heart of the pension program lay the "suitable home" policy. In order to be eligible to receive pensions, mothers had to be widowed, divorced, deserted, separated, unmarried, or married to imprisoned, ill, or handicapped husbands. In addition, and most important, mothers had to be judged physically, morally, and mentally fit to have custody of their children. Bell (1965) observed that "the state and the mother entered a partnership, as it were, in which both parties assumed certain responsibilities directed toward ensuring that a small group of needy children would remain in their own homes and be so supervised and educated as to become

Culver

A preschool program in New York City's Grand Street Settlement House, 1938.

assets, not liabilities, to a democratic society" (p. 5). "The question of giving relief depends in part at least upon the character of the mother, upon her ability to maintain a good home, and upon her willingness to cooperate in plans that mean proper care for the family" (Wright, 1922, p. 81). In exchange for the pension, mothers were expected to maintain suitable homes, be devoted and competent child rearers, and uphold proper moral standards for the children.

In spite of the rapid spread of the mothers' pensions program through some portions of the country, many counties refused to endorse it. Pensions reached only a small fraction of the families who needed them. Local legislation of pensions remained optional, and federal guidelines for their administration were not constructed until the 1935 enactment of Social Security, establishing ADC. Local grants varied widely. In most states payments were not adequate, and many recipients were forced to work part-time as domestics to supplement their grants (Leff, 1973, pp. 413–414). The Children's Bureau estimated that more than twice as many children were eligible for aid than received it (Bradbury, 1962/1974, p. 36). Judgments concerning worthiness were sometimes fickle and at other times plainly discriminatory. Blacks in particular faced discrimination—receiving only 3% of the total pensions and with a number of counties and some Southern states barring Blacks totally from their programs (Leff, 1973, p. 414).

The advent of mothers' pensions delivered a staggering blow to the day nursery movement—a blow, however, that did not entirely eclipse the movement. At the height of pension activities in 1916, 695 day nurseries were operating, sponsored by charitable organizations. By 1921 the number had fallen to around 500 in spite of a continuing trend for mothers to work outside the home (Tank, 1980, p. 152).

In cases where the family did not qualify for pensions or where pensions were inadequate, the demand for day nursery care persisted, and such care remained available. However, those families who resorted to day nursery services because they were rejected from the pensions program were stigmatized as the "unworthy" poor. The progressive priority "was to keep the good mother at home with her children, not to supervise the children in centers while the women worked" (Rothman, 1973, pp. 16–17).

THE 1920s AND 1930s: THE PROFESSIONS AND CHILDREN

The emergence, in the 1920s and 1930s, of child psychology as a respectable academic enterprise was due in no small measure to the generosity of philanthropists. During this time, the Laura Spelman Rockefeller Memorial Foundation awarded significant sums of money to several universities and colleges in order to establish child study institutes (Lomax, 1977; Cravens, 1985; Schlossman, 1981). Some of the many activities undertaken included research on child development, training in parent education, and training for early childhood education. At the center of the institutes was the nursery school, which provided at one and the same time a laboratory for research on child development and an enrichment program for the children enrolled. As parent education programs proliferated in and around the institutes, American parents became increasingly convinced that the modern family required expert, scientific guidance from professionals to encourage healthy child development. And while the nursery school found some advocates among a handful of social altruists who sought to make it available to poor families, it was most popular among child psychologists, educators, and affluent families.

New expertise also affected poverty-track day nurseries after World War I. The decline in day nurseries in the second decade of this century was followed by a series of important changes in their administration and perceived purpose. At the same time, a series of developments within the social work profession carried a very different set of effects for the care of the poor preschool child. First, social workers became increasingly involved in administering the newly emerging social welfare system. Second, social work shifted away from its earlier association with social reform toward a more psychological and clinical perspective on social welfare. Specifically, social workers adopted casework methods of family diagnosis based on clinical psychology. The professional social worker aspired to use the day nursery only as a temporary expedient in the process of helping poor families return to the mainstream of American life—a world in which the father worked outside the home and the mother of young children stayed home. Thus, the newly professionalized social workers reinforced the growing stigmatization of out-of-home child care for children of working poor parents. As a result of these (and other) changes, the day nursery was regarded as a viable but not uncritically accepted element within the emerging social welfare system.

The Nursery School

Nursery school activities were designed to provide children with an opportunity to develop socially through association with their peers under the expert supervision of a trained teacher. Through group play activities, children ranging in age from 2 to 4 would learn to respect the rights of others, assert their own rights, use language as a means of communication, and cooperate with other children. "By sharing his play materials and equipment, maintaining his own rights, obeying authority, practicing self-control in waiting his turn, and being helpful, the child learns to meet many social responsibilities" (Whipple, 1929, p. 180). The nursery school was a place where the individualism fostered at home might be tempered by an emphasis on the requirements of collective life. According to this view, participation in nursery school classes provided an unparalleled opportunity for children—especially only children—to interact with other young children in an environment that promoted normal social development.

Second, nursery schools emphasized the motor skills, sensory discrimination, and physical growth of young children. These sorts of physical aspects of development ranked second in developmental significance only to the child's "successful adjustment to the social situation" (Whipple, 1929, p. 182). A third emphasis of the nursery school was to promote and maintain child health. The nursery school was to be "ever watchful of the health of the children in its care" (Wolf, 1933, p. 268). Nursery schools frequently worked in consultation with, and in some cases employed, professional dieticians, pediatricians, nurses, psychologists, and social workers.

Like the day nursery during the time that mothers' pensions were

"Nursery schools catered almost exclusively to children of the middle and upper classes. In short, the nursery school persisted as a track for affluent parents and their children."

introduced, the nursery school was criticized for taking the child away from the mother, thereby disrupting the relationship between mother and child, and was perceived by some as a threat to family cohesion and social stability. Sensitive to these criticisms, advocates maintained that nursery school experience would strengthen rather than weaken parent-child relationships. Helen Woolley, for example, argued that the separation provided in the nursery school "improved the emotional relationship between mother and child and enhanced its value" (Woolley, 1926, p. 295). Advocates stressed that the nursery school did not replace but rather supplemented the home.

In sum, the nursery school attempted to reach the "whole child." Its central aim was to create an environment for young children that promoted wholesome social and emotional development, enhanced physical growth, and safeguarded mental and physical health. Most nursery schools assumed a broad perspective in their efforts to teach children a wide range of behaviors and promote their general well-being.

The Nursery School in Context

Some educators advocated nursery schools in response to a perceived decline in the quality of family life after World War I. "The modern home," wrote one critic of postwar family life, "is lacking in equipment for the upbringing of young children and needs to be supplemented. The supplementing of home education for young children by educational experts thus becomes an important task of the educational system" (Merrill Palmer School, 1921, p. 1). Similarly, William F. Russell, dean of Teachers College at Columbia University, noted that the home, the neighborhood, and the church had "weakened" and that the school was obliged to intervene in the socialization of young children. Because of the change in status of the home, Russell believed, it "now [failed] to do what it once did" (Russell, 1931, p. 9). He called for the downward extension of education to the nursery school as a means of compensating for the decline in the capacity of the family to socialize its children. "The nursery school," he advised, "is one of the efforts made by society to compensate for this defect; and parental education is one way of trying to rehabilitate the institution [of the family] which cannot do its share" (p. 9). In the wake of recent research in medicine and psychology, many felt that traditional approaches to child rearing were no longer adequate. "The home is rare," one mother wrote, "which provides the companionship, the equipment, and the scientific care suited to American needs" (Hidden, 1927, p. 463). Educated mothers, with the time available and money to spend, turned to nursery education to help provide the child care and child-rearing advice they thought they needed. With their children in nursery school, affluent parents could rest assured that their children were receiving "the most intelligent care available" and the best child-rearing advice (Whipple, 1929, p. 147).

Other aspects of contemporary family life also fueled the nursery school movement. Urban life-styles—tenement and apartment living— often meant that children went without adequate space for play and recreation. Some felt that the urban environment deprived children of the means to satisfy their curiosity and to fulfill their desire to play by exploring the "natural playground that was the back lot, neighborhood, or farm" (cited in Tank, 1980, p. 282). Further, the mobility associated with urban life made some observers feel that city children were robbed of the companionship and guidance of the extended family. Thus, proponents argued that nursery schools were the best means of caring for children in large cities.

A new generation of college-educated women was also attracted to the nursery school as a vocation in itself. Participation in the child development movement—whether it took the form of studying child development in a child study institute, teaching nursery school, or participating in parent education courses—represented a middle ground for a generation of women seeking to combine marriage with the challenge, purpose, and intellectual vitality they had come to value in their college experience.

By the late 1920s, the nursery school had become a center for preparing "women to meet the responsibilities of family life and the obligations of parenthood" (Whipple, 1929, p. 28). In 1931, 74 American colleges and universities sponsored nursery schools. Sixty-six institutions of higher learning reported that research in child development was the primary function of their nursery school. In the same year, teacher education programs in 47 colleges or universities reported using the nursery school for the purposes of professional training for teachers (Davis & Hansen, 1933, p. 31). Clearly, early childhood education achieved a new professionalism in these years.

The nursery school obviously filled a need among groups of child development researchers, childhood educators, parent educators, middle- and upper-class parents, and a small number of social workers. It failed, however, to gain broad-based support. By 1932 not more than 500 nursery schools had been established in the country. These schools enrolled between 10,000 and 14,000 children (Tank, 1980, p. 294). Only a tiny fraction of the nation's approximately 16 million preschoolers actually benefited from nursery school. Nursery schools catered almost exclusively to children of the middle and upper classes. In short, the nursery school persisted as a track for affluent parents and their children.

Just as it is beginning to be revealed that Blacks sponsored day nurseries separate from those of whites, so some evidence suggests the existence of a child development movement among Blacks in these years—a movement parallel to and independent from that of whites (Cunningham & Osborn, 1979). Like the white movement, the Black child development movement centered itself around colleges and universities. Laboratory nursery schools opened at Hampton Institute and Spelman College in 1929 and 1930. In 1931, Flemmie Kittrell, the first Black to receive a doctorate in early childhood education, opened a laboratory nursery school attached to Bennett College (Cunningham and Osborn, 1979). Billingsley and Giovannoni (1972) indicate that Black efforts in both the kindergarten and nursery fields were notable attempts to enrich rather than merely maintain children.

The New Profession of Social Work and the Day Nursery

While the expertise surrounding nursery schools came largely from university-based child development researchers, the expertise that was to influence the day nursery emanated from social work. As the professionalization of social work proceeded and brought social casework techniques to bear on the "pathologies" of the poor, the influence of social work on the day nursery became more visible. At the 1919 National Conference of Social Work, Grace Caldwell outlined the relationship between the day nursery and the newly professionalized field of social work. Caldwell advised that, as with any other social welfare service, admission to the day nursery should follow only after the completion of a full investigation of the family by a trained social caseworker. Of signal importance to the question of a child's admission to a day nursery was the question of whether nursery services would "help eliminate the underlying causes of social maladjustment" (Caldwell, 1919, p. 44). Such "adjustment" problems were presumed to underlie a family's need for day nursery services. Problems in family

> *"As early as 1940, the National Association*
> *of Day Nurseries warned that existing day-care*
> *facilities would be inadequate if mothers*
> *entered into the war production*
> *effort in large numbers."*

adjustment both disrupted family life and required the mother to enter the work force, thereby creating the need for the services of a day nursery.

The framework of "social pathology," "maladjustment of the family," "social maladjustment," "right social diagnosis," and "constructive case work" all reveal the extent to which day nursery service became a part of a psychologically oriented social welfare system. This social welfare system was intended to help the poor who were thought to be overwhelmed not so much by economic problems as problems of social and personal adjustment. Participants in the 1931 White House Conference on Child Health and Protection asserted that the heart of day nursery work was the application of "good social casework to problem families. Each child should be studied in light of how his mother may best care for him, and plans for him should involve concern and responsibility for the well-being of the entire family" (White House Conference, 1931, p. 14). While remaining under the auspices of social welfare, day nurseries became a last resort in the care of young children whose mothers worked.

Finally, the establishment of ADC in 1935 diminished the demand for day nursery services by emphasizing grants-in-aid rather than employment as a means of helping poor families. The passage of this act marked a new era in the history of public welfare in the United States—an era during which state and federal governments entered into a partnership to finance, operate, and administer local programs devised to aid needy children in their own homes. Like mothers' pensions, cash payments allowed mothers who were deprived of the support of a husband to remain at home with their children (Bell, 1965, pp. 20–39). Just as mothers' pensions programs did not eliminate the need for day nurseries, so the inadequacy of ADC ensured the persistence of day nurseries.

The Day Nursery in the 1920s: Attempts to Raise Standards of Care

As the influence of preschool education spread out from universities and research institutions in the 1920s and 1930s, a growing number of day nurseries tried to focus attention on the education and development of the preschool child. These attempts by day nurseries to emulate the nursery schools led to the reduction of teacher-child ratios, the acquisition of more and better equipment, the use of a coherent pedagogical component, and other innovations. In an effort, for example, to "furnish a natural educative environment to develop the activity side of the child," the Day Nursery Association of Milwaukee organized a pedagogical program "to provide the right kind of conditions for the development of the physical, mental, and emotional phases of child life" (cited in Tank, 1980, p. 316). Thus the nursery school movement did have a positive influence on the day nursery, both through the publication of research findings and the placement of trained nursery school teachers in some day nurseries (Beer, 1957, p. 48). While the precipitating need for day nursery care remained maternal employment, an increasing number of day nursery workers attempted to imitate the multifaceted approach of the middle-class nursery schools. Some even hoped to use the day nursery as a kind of compensatory program, much the way Head Start is used today. Day nurseries offering programs along the lines of nursery schools could properly boast to critics that poor children in the day nursery were receiving experiences comparable to those of middle-class children in nursery school. In the 1920s "day nurseries offering a preschool educational program found a new raison d'être through providing educational advantages to the very young children of the less favored economic classes" (Forest, 1927, p. 320).

For lack of resources, however, relatively few day nurseries were able to respond in such a positive fashion to the nursery school model. A 1924 survey of 149 day nurseries selected as being "the best in the country as far as the National Federation of Day Nurseries knew" revealed that only 57% of the nurseries conducted any sort of prekindergarten, Montessori, or nursery school programs (Anon., 1924, p. 230). In her 1924 survey of day nurseries in Pennsylvania, Helen Tyson found that the "time is too short, the workers too few" to do much in the way of educational work except for some training in health habits and table manners (Tyson, 1925, p. 24). The question of custodial care versus "developmental" care or enrichment again rested on economic considerations.

A Brief Campaign for Licensure

There were serious reasons for attempting to improve the health conditions of many day nurseries. Surveys of day nurseries in Pennsylvania, New York City, and Chicago revealed that most centers did not achieve modern standards of child hygiene, health care, or nutrition (Wright, 1922, pp. 18–20). In the mid-1920s children's advocates launched a campaign to raise day nursery standards by means of state regulation. "The only safety lies in compulsory regulation" wrote one social worker "with the department of health or welfare operating a licensing system to enforce minimum standards as well as safeguard the mental, moral, and physical health of every child involved" (Colbourne, 1924, p. 396). Another advocate wrote:

> Public-health authorities should not lose the opportunity to reach children of the preschool age group. Day nurseries should be maintained under proper and competent supervision, which could best be carried out by government authorities. For this reason all communities should include in their public health laws provision that no nursery shall be conducted without a permit therefore, issued by the local board of health or otherwise than in accordance with such regulations as the said board of health may issue from time to time. (Baker, 1919, p. 220)

The campaign for licensure was only partially successful. By the time of the depression, most of the approximately 800 day nurseries in the United States were subject to some form of public regulation. However, there is reason to believe that "ordinances were not strictly enforced" (Wright, 1922, p. 18).

An Argument over Infant Care

As part of the generally heightened concern over day nursery standards in the 1920s, renewed debates took place on the advisability of accepting infants into the nursery. Day nurseries had traditionally cared for infants as young as 10 days old. The debate over infant care was fueled by a battle between public health experts promoting bottle-feeding under more sanitary conditions and psychologists arguing persuasively in favor of breast-feeding. In 1910, Dr. Carolyn Hedger, addressing the National Federation of Day Nurseries, asserted that "it takes mother-love, mother arms, mother breasts and considerable common sense to grow a human properly for the first nine months and no institution, no matter how scientific, how philanthropic, can replace these things" (National Federation of Day Nurseries, 1922, p. 28). Again in 1919—this time before the National Conference of Social Work—she argued that breast feeding was the foundation of infant health and "no child under nine months should be deprived of this" (Hedger, 1919, p. 46). Finally, Hedger declared, since "we shall never have the right to interrupt breast-feeding," nurseries should admit only children older than 9 months of age (p. 46). By the mid-1920s most of the better day nurseries refused to admit infants under the age of nine months. A social worker

A day care program in a housing project in Queens, New York, 1942.

Culver

writing for the National Federation of Day Nurseries stated that "the placement of a baby under one year of age in the nursery to enable the mother to work raises serious questions connected with the welfare of the mother and the child and whenever possible should be avoided" (National Federation of Day Nurseries, 1922, p. 28). Efforts to remove infants from the day nurseries, however, were always measured against the alternative—that babies might be left to indifferent care or worse.

Throughout the 1920s, early childhood education, socialization, and care remained the primary responsibility of the family. Despite the efforts of slowly emerging social and welfare services, most communities continued to hold the family almost solely responsible for the health, education, and welfare of its young children.

The federal government continued to uphold its 1909 declaration made at the First White House Conference on Children. During that conference, private organizations, local governments, and welfare agencies were encouraged to construct programs to safeguard the welfare of children and to strengthen the family. Public activities on behalf of children remained circumscribed because of the long-standing ideological commitment to child rearing as the singular responsibility of the private nuclear family. The primacy of federal nonintervention in family policy was set aside in the 1930s and 1940s in response to two crises—one was economic and the other a matter of national defense.

THE FEDERAL ROLE: A SERIES OF CRISIS INTERVENTIONS

In response to the economic crisis of the depression, Congress earmarked $6 million for the establishment of emergency nursery schools. The primary purpose of these Works Progress Administration (WPA) nursery schools was to provide work for unemployed teachers, custodians, cooks, and nurses. Only secondarily were these nurseries established to serve needy young children.

While the emergency nursery schools were later dismantled as the nation prepared for war in the 1940s, national labor needs led to the establishment, under the Lanham Act, of over 3,000 child care centers to care for children whose mothers worked in defense-related industries. Like the WPA nurseries, these federally sponsored child care centers were established in response to a national emergency. But, unlike the emergency nursery schools that admitted only children from poor families, Lanham Act centers served children and families regardless of socioeconomic status. Such widespread support for the nation's children was short-lived. The Lanham Act centers were a "win-the-war," not a "save-the-child," program. Funds were withdrawn shortly after the war's end.

Child Care during the Depression

When President Roosevelt took office in March 1933, his "New Deal for the American people" initiated programs that would leave few aspects of American life untouched. As a part of the government's new willingness to accept at least partial responsibility for the welfare of the unemployed worker, Congress authorized a half-billion dollars in relief money to be channeled through state and local agencies by the Federal Emergency Relief Administration (FERA).

Led by Harry Hopkins, FERA was charged with meeting the special needs of several groups, including unemployed teachers, nurses, service workers, and preschool children from underprivileged homes (Hopkins, 1936). Hopkins authorized the establishment of emergency nursery schools as one of several branches of the Federal Emergency Education program. Although there was no initial mention of nursery schools, on September 6, 1933, Jacob Baker, assistant administrator of FERA, wrote to Grace Abbott, director of the Children's Bureau, on behalf of a number of observers who saw a link between the needs of unemployed teachers and the effects of the depression on young children. Baker sought Abbott's cooperation with FERA in establishing emergency nursery schools. On October 23, 1933,

"Communities that did apply for . . . funds faced a bureaucratic maze in which no fewer than seven different agencies were involved in allocating funds."

State Emergency Relief administrators were notified by Hopkins that "the rules and regulations of the Federal Emergency Relief Administration may be interpreted to provide work relief wages for qualified and unemployed teachers and other workers on relief who are needed to organize and conduct nursery schools under the control of the public school systems" (National Advisory Committee, 1934, p. 8).

During the winter of 1933–34, emergency nursery schools were launched under the auspices of FERA and were incorporated into the WPA in 1934 when FERA was terminated. Consistent with the policy of safeguarding the "physical and mental well-being of preschool children from needy, under-privileged families," any child between the ages of 2 and 5 whose family was on relief was eligible to attend an emergency nursery school (National Advisory Committee, 1935, p. 16). In any one year, between 44,000 and 72,000 children were enrolled—serving a mere fraction of the 10 million preschoolers with unemployed fathers (p. 356).

Of the 6,000 to 8,000 persons employed by the emergency nursery schools, approximately 51% were teachers, 12% were nurses, 17% were nutritionists and cooks, and the remainder were janitors, clerks, maids, and other service workers. The schools were planned and initiated by local governments and typically operated under the joint auspices of state departments of education and local public school systems.

While the principal reason for establishing these nursery schools was to create jobs for the unemployed, Hopkins did acknowledge that "the educational and health programs of nursery schools can aid as nothing else in combating the physical and mental handicaps being imposed upon these young children in the homes of needy and unemployed parents" (Langdon, 1938, p. 472). Through the cooperation of early childhood educators, social workers, physicians, and public health officials, these emergency nursery schools were intended to mitigate some of the misery surrounding children during the depression by providing thousands of them with the "opportunity for wholesome development, for better living" (Department of Education, 1936, p. 34). However, the schools were neither day nurseries for children of the working poor nor progressive nursery schools. Rather, they were "poverty track institutions designed to safeguard the health and welfare of impoverished preschool children during very hard times" (Tank, 1980, p. 359).

Activities of the Depression Emergency Nursery Schools

Emergency nursery schools placed their first priority on maintaining child health and welfare. In addition to food, rest, and preventive medicine, children attending emergency nursery schools were also provided with an opportunity to play under safe and healthful conditions. And while the health and dietary programs in some emergency nursery schools "were below any desirable standards . . . first hand inspection of many nursery schools revealed that they accomplished a great deal in improving the nutrition, health supervision, and medical service of the children enrolled" (Stoddard, 1934, p. 194).

With an average teacher-child ratio of 1:19, emergency nursery schools could not provide the individualized attention that characterized the traditional nursery school. Their emphasis lay on meeting the basic health and nutritional requirements of young children. Consequently, emergency nursery schools were limited to providing minimal sorts of custodial care. When one considers the conditions and limited resources with which these programs were created—to provide for work relief and child welfare to ease the burdens of an economic crisis—one should not be surprised by the imperative to focus on meeting basic needs of the children. In sum, emergency nursery schools served to shelter the young children of families that were on relief from the want and insecurity associated with the depression.

In spite of limited resources, some emergency nursery schools introduced parent education programs—a practice usually limited to the traditional nursery school. A spokesman for the schools noted that "what happens to the child becomes a matter of concern since much of the advantage gained by attending nursery school will be lost unless its principles of child care can be carried over into the remainder of the child's life" (cited in Tank, 1980, p. 368). Teachers would visit the homes of children to confer with parents; parents were invited to visit the nursery school in order to "learn more about how they can guide their child's growth and development" (p. 368).

In the final analysis, emergency nursery schools represented a small-scale effort to save children from some of the burdens of an economic crisis. Part of the federal government's response to this crisis was to provide limited backing to a relatively small, temporary (though innovative) relief program serving children and unemployed workers. The narrow scope, uneven quality, and limited availability of health, nutrition, and child care services of the emergency nursery schools again reflect the nation's ambivalent attitudes toward both the poor and government-supported child care outside the home.

Child Care During World War II

When World War II broke out in Europe, the economic crisis in the United States gave way to a national war emergency. With the precipitous drop in unemployment ushered in by the war, the problems of relief and the need for emergency nursery schools also diminished. However, when labor needs in the defense industries required the employment of 1.5 million mothers with preschool children, the federal government once again ventured into child care.

During the course of the war, the number of working women increased by more than 50% to bring the total number above 6 million. The services of women became central to the successful management of the war effort at home. When the United States entered the war, fewer than 1 out of 30 mothers with preschool children worked. By war's end, nearly 1 mother out of 8 with children under 6 was employed (Chafe, 1972). Hundreds of thousands of newly employed mothers thus experienced firsthand the problems associated with working outside the home, running a household, and taking care of children.

With the rise in maternal employment, absenteeism and job turnover quickly became significant problems in the workplace. A survey made at a Michigan defense plant revealed that 15% of its employed mothers missed work periodically because of problems arranging child care (U.S. Congress, 1943, p. 48). In his analysis of the woman's role in the war, Chafe claimed that "approximately 20% of all female absenteeism was due to the need to supervise infant and school age youngsters" (Chafe, 1972, p. 162). Nationwide, the War Manpower Commission estimated that as many as 2 million children needed some form of nonparental child care. In addition to contributing to absenteeism and turnover, the lack of child care facilities prevented thousands of unemployed mothers from joining the domestic war effort.

Large numbers of children with mothers working toward the war effort were not receiving adequate care. Newspapers and magazines reported stories of young children who were left with unstable guardians, in parked cars, or who were injured in accidents in unsupervised homes (Anon., 1942,

p. 21). One such account detailed the story of how nine children and four dogs were found locked in their home while the parents worked all day in a factory in Southern California. Another account revealed how four young children were found harnessed to a post while their mother worked in a defense plant (Close, 1943, p. 194).

In a few cases industry made innovative strides toward alleviating the child care shortage. Some few defense companies supported child care programs to meet their employment and production needs. The best-known of such programs was sponsored by the Kaiser Shipbuilding Company. Using $750,000 in federal funds appropriated by the U.S. Maritime Commission, Kaiser established 24-hour child care centers for children from 18 months to 6 years of age. Included among the many features of these high-quality centers were long and flexible operating hours, skilled and well-paid staff, close proximity to the production plants, and provision for take-out meals (Tank, 1980, p. 375). Although considered to be models of their kind, the Kaiser child care centers were not widely imitated.

As early as 1940, the National Association of Day Nurseries warned that existing day-care facilities would be inadequate if mothers entered into the war production effort in large numbers. Federal aid however, would not be forthcoming until mid-1943. In the meantime, communities did the best they could with limited resources. Early in the war, government agencies recommended to employers that mothers with children under 14 should not be recruited for work unless all other labor sources had been exhausted. Paul McNutt, head of the War Manpower Commission, stated in July 1942 that as a matter of policy "the first responsibility of women with young children, in war as in peace, is to give suitable care in their own homes to their children" (cited in Tank, 1980, p. 379). The chief of the Children's Bureau continued to believe that during the war, as during peacetime, a "mother's primary duty is to her home. This duty is one she cannot lay aside, no matter what the emergency" (cited in Chafe, 1972, p. 164). Similarly, Frances Perkins, secretary of labor, noted in 1942 that "in this time of crisis . . . mothers of young children can make no finer contribution to the strength of the nation and its vitality and effectiveness in the future than to assure their children the security of home, individual care, and affections" (Child Welfare League, 1942, p. 7). In the same spirit, a journalist observed that "no informed American needs a psychologist to tell him that children separated from their home ties and without constant care . . . are the troublemakers, the neurotics, and the spiritual and emotional cripples of a generation hence" (Child Welfare League, 1942, p. 7).

Many mothers felt reluctant to send their children to existing day-care

"The effects of day care on young children's attachment and social behavior remain an influential and highly disputed area of research and policy."

centers. When asked in a Gallup poll in 1943 whether they would accept a job in a war plant if their children were to receive child care free of charge, only 29% of the mothers polled replied yes while 56% replied no (Cantrel, 1951, p. 1046). One mother asked, "Why should I put my children in a place where they're lined up from morning till night?" Another mother commented that "child care centers are all right for charity cases; but my children belong at home" (Baruch, 1943, p. 254). The historical association of day care with relief worked against the acceptance of community child care facilities even during the war. Many mothers expressed dismay at the idea of placing their children in the care of strangers, preferring that they be cared for by a relative, friend, or neighbor. In 10 cities studied by the Women's Bureau, only 5% of the mothers sampled decided to place their children in a day nursery while 71% made arrangements with a relative or neighbor to care for their children (cited in Tank, 1980, p. 381).

When the war began, most of the 1,700 WPA emergency nursery schools were still in operation. By 1942 most of these centers faced imminent closing due to the lack of people eligible for WPA employment. In July 1942, Congress authorized the use of $6 million of the WPA appropriation for use to provide child care facilities for children of working mothers. Congress also authorized an extension in hours, the employment of nonrelief personnel, and the establishment of new facilities to meet emergency day-care needs. By the end of May 1943, 1,150 of the 1,700 WPA nursery schools were operating in war-disrupted areas serving children and families regardless of income. For most of the 550 WPA emergency nursery schools not located in such areas, there was no prospect of reopening (Close, 1943, p. 195; Bond, 1945, p. 55).

With the liquidation of the WPA in 1943, the operation of emergency nursery schools located in defense production areas continued with the aid of Lanham Act funds. Besieged by requests for child care facilities, the administration authorized, in August 1942, that money originally allocated to housing and public works could be used on a matching basis to establish emergency day-care centers in war-disrupted areas. By the end of 1943, the six Lanham Act grants had been approved. By February 1944, the Federal

Works Administration (FWA) reported 2,243 centers serving 65,772 children. Shortly thereafter, President Roosevelt released $400,000 from the emergency war fund for the purpose of "promoting, stimulating, and coordinating day care programs for the children of working mothers" (Tank, 1980, p. 384). Funds were to be used to advise local communities and supervise state initiatives; funds were not to be used for actual operating costs. The same day Roosevelt made the money available, he wrote to a FWA official: "I do not believe that further federal funds should be provided for actual operation of child care programs at this time" (cited in Chafe, 1972, pp. 299–300, n.33).

Roosevelt's refusal to fund operating costs reflected once again the government's ambivalence toward providing child care. Funds were distributed only to those communities engaged in defense production in which there existed a shortage of child care facilities. Funds for those facilities would be terminated with the end of the war. One FWA official said that funds were allotted "solely as a war emergency measure in order to facilitate the employment of women needed in the war. We are not substituting an expanded educational program nor a federal welfare program, but we are making money available to assist local communities in meeting a war need for the care of children while their mothers are engaged in war production" (U.S. Congress, 1943, p. 34). Clearly the federally funded child care centers were "an answer to a war problem" (Wetherill, 1943, p. 634) and in no way indicated an eclipse of traditional ideological commitments regarding the place of women and children in the home.

By the time the administration acted, the child care problem had reached crisis proportions. At the height of the Lanham Act program's effectiveness in July 1944, 3,102 centers were in operation, serving 129,357 children. Government estimates had suggested the need for federal assistance to provide for 1 million children. Hence, even at the height of the program, a mere 13% of children in need of care received federal assistance. Cities such as New York were not eligible for funds because it was not considered a war-disrupted area. The federal matching requirements, as well as a further requirement that communities refund to the government any funds not used by the end of the year, discouraged many communities from undertaking such a controversial program. As a result, few of them even sought Lanham funds to expand child care facilities.

Communities that did apply for Lanham funds faced a bureaucratic maze in which no fewer than seven different agencies were involved in allocating funds. One state official remarked that his efforts to apply and secure funds were "pretty much like a horse forever dancing around at his starting place," and an exasperated children's advocate concluded that the Lanham Act "delayed more than it furthered" the establishment of day-care facilities (cited in Chafe, 1972, pp. 166,167).

Once established, federally funded child care centers confronted still more difficulties. Limited budgets implied a lack of suitable physical space, a shortage of adequate personnel, and inadequate medical supervision. Many centers were located in inappropriate and undesirable settings—buildings and rooms ill fitted for use by young children. Efforts to provide quality child care were also hindered in too many cases by a shortage of qualified teachers, nurses, and administrators as well as a general lack of standards for salaries, qualifications, hours, and working conditions.

In locations where private or local funds supplemented federal money, the quality of child care was often good. A number of communities were able to convert federal housing projects, settlements, school buildings, or churches into well-equipped child care centers. Those communities with more funds were also able to maintain higher personnel and medical standards.

In 1943 FWA came under attack from the Federal Security Administration (FSA), an amalgam of social welfare departments including the Office of Education and the Children's Bureau. At the core of their criticisms lay the charge that FWA viewed federal child care as a temporary expedient and paid small heed to the welfare of the nation's children (Tank, 1980, p. 392). FSA, reflecting the attitudes of children's advocates, was not about to stand by while FWA constructed a nationwide chain of "baby parking stations" (p. 393). FSA rallied for foster care for children under 2 and attempted to gain control of a program whose management they perceived as lying with a group of engineers who knew little about children. Their efforts failed. Control of the child care centers continued to rest with FWA and problems continued to surround existing centers. As during the depression, the federal government's attitude during the war toward becoming involved in the care and education of the preschool child was ambivalent at best.

A Postwar Return to Normalcy

The federal government's commitment to child care ended with the end of hostilities. A "return to normalcy" became possible after the war. Mothers returned home from work, and fathers returned from war to work outside the home. Since the Lanham Act centers had been created by an administrative decision and not by Congress, their dismantling was easily accomplished. Late in August 1945, an FWA official stated that "since the

A Catholic day nursery in Harlem, New York City, 1947.

Culver

assistance under the Lanham Act for child care and civilian recreation had been based on the recruitment and retention of workers for war production and essential supporting services, funding for federal child care would be terminated as soon as practicable" (Anon., 1946, p. 10). Protests against the curtailment of child care services flooded the offices of President Truman, FWA and members of Congress. In response to such pressure, President Truman requested that Congress earmark $7 million for child care projects through March 1, 1946. The president wrote to Congress:

> The conversion of the wartime child-care program to peacetime operations under which the local communities would assume the financial responsibility requires federal assistance for a few more months. This extension of time would give working mothers more time to make other arrangements for the care of their children. (Anon., 1945, p. 13)

Congress approved the extension of federal money for child care only with the assurance that such aid was temporary.

While federal funds for child care terminated at the end of the war, many mothers with preschool children continued to work outside the home. The war experience had demonstrated women's capability to perform a wide assortment of tasks traditionally associated with men's work. The war also made it possible for large numbers of women to combine motherhood and work (Chafe, 1972, p. 155).

By the late 1950s, 2.9 million mothers with preschool children were employed and confronted the problem of child care (Myrdal & Klein, 1968, p. 64). Those families in which the mother worked continued to rely on traditional sources of child care—relatives, friends, or neighbors in a family setting. A 1958 Children's Bureau study revealed that 94% of the more than 2 million preschool children were cared for in their own or someone else's home while their mothers worked. One percent went without adult supervision, and only four percent received group care in a day nursery, day-care center, settlement house, or nursery school (Lajewski, 1959, pp. 14–22).

Group child care during the late 1940s and 1950s remained unpopular. Willard Waller (1945), a Barnard sociologist, contended that the very survival of the home was threatened because working mothers were not able to fulfill their maternal responsibilities during the war. For Waller and many others as well, the solution was to restore the traditional nuclear family in which the father worked outside the home and the mother remained home to take care of their children. Dr. Benjamin Spock also urged mothers to forgo employment during the preschool years for the sake of the children and the family. Spock declared in both the 1947 and 1958 editions of *Baby and Child Care* that "useful and well-adjusted citizens are the most valuable possessions a country has, and good mother care during the earliest childhood is the surest way to produce them. It doesn't make sense to let mothers go to work making dresses or tapping typewriters in an office, and have them pay other people to do a poorer job of bringing up their own children" (cited in Grubb & Lazerson, 1982, p. 34).

In the field of child development, observations of children during a period when only mothers cared for their children led to normative prescriptions that mothers were the best parents, and to warnings of the dire consequences for children whose mothers worked. At the same time, a large popular literature appeared—based largely on a series of papers written by René Spitz in the mid-1940s—describing the devastating effects of institutionalization on orphans. The babies observed by Spitz suffered from inconsistent care and spent most of their days staring vacantly at the ceiling. They were apathetic and showed high rates of morbidity. Spitz (1945; 1946) concluded, and those hostile to day care agreed, that the anomalous development of these babies was due to their lack of attachment to a specific caretaker. Other aspects of the babies' experiences were ignored, and generalizations about the effects of day care were made from the literature on this group of severely deprived babies. Spitz's conclusions were made even more accessible to the public through John Bowlby's World Health Organization Report, *Maternal Care and Mental Health* (1951). Although the original research was conducted with institutionalized children, psychologists and others were quick to generalize Spitz's findings to family settings and conclude that young children should not be separated from their mothers. The effects of day care on young children's attachment and social behavior remain an influential and highly disputatious area of research and policy (c.f. Belsky, 1988; Gamble & Zigler, 1986; Scarr, 1984).

In the 1950s day care continued to be perceived and administered as a social welfare service. The task of the caseworker was to coordinate child care with other social welfare services in order to help parents meet their "full parental rights and responsibilities" (Ruderman, 1968, pp. 12-17). Where publicly supported day care survived the termination of Lanham Act funds, it was sponsored by social welfare agencies. Centers established with public funds in the District of Columbia, for example, were established for the exclusive use of children of low-income employed parents with the hope that child care provisions would enable poor mothers to get off of welfare rolls and onto payrolls (Steiner, 1976, p. 18). Philadelphia's publicly funded day care centers, although administered by the city's Board of Education, were intended primarily to strengthen the family life of the working poor and to help prevent juvenile delinquency. Local social workers justified the public expenditure of funds for day care by claiming that it was a means of enabling mothers to work in such a way as to reduce the welfare burden. And New York State's brief experiment with publicly funded child care ended in 1947 when Governor Thomas E. Dewey terminated state support for day care and called those who protested the decision "Communists" (Steiner, 1976, p. 18).

With both state and municipal funding, child care in postwar New York City remained a social welfare program for the poor. Employees of the welfare department were required to investigate each applicant and to separate out those who were not deemed needy of assistance or work. Mothers wishing to place their children in a publicly supported day-care center were required to submit to a means test to establish their level of need for public assistance. Steiner comments that in California, where centers originally established under the Lanham Act still survive, the program "has been sustained through most of its life as a way of freeing low-income mothers from actual or potential dependence on welfare assistance" (Steiner, 1976, p. 20). In general, as in the prewar years, most working mothers with preschool children made informal child care arrangements with relatives, friends, or neighbors. Few families in the American mainstream relied on group care—regarded by most as appropriate only for "problem" children from "marginal" homes (Tank, 1980, p. 422).

Early childhood education underwent few changes between the 1920s and the 1950s. Nursery school education continued to stress "the full development of the young child and the successful functioning of the child within the group" (Moustakas & Berson, 1955, p. 17); nursery schools continued to emphasize that their function was to supplement, not supplant, the family's own socialization activities. The distinction between supplemental nursery school for the affluent and custodial day care for the poor persisted through these decades.

ENTERING THE 1960s: A COINCIDENCE OF FORCES

Beginning in the 1960s and continuing through the 1970s, institutions for the preschool child changed dramatically in the wake of social changes and intellectual challenges. In the 1960s new ideas about child development led to a series of changes in program content and a rapid growth of interest in early childhood education. Educators in this area had traditionally placed little emphasis on intellectual development; in fact, many consciously steered clear of the intellectual aspects of development. Widely held views concerning the effects of early experience on later personality development, and traditional ideas concerning intelligence as both fixed and inherited combined to keep out of the nursery school an emphasis on cognitive development.

Research conducted in the 1950s and 1960s challenged the notion of the immutability of intelligence by suggesting that certain kinds of experiences may affect the rate of early cognitive development. In 1961, J. McVicker Hunt published *Intelligence and Experience*—a book that was to be extremely influential. Hunt asserted that the early years play a significant role in providing the foundation for later learning. Hunt thus implied that the preschool years were much more important for intellectual development than previously thought. In 1964, Benjamin Bloom published *Stability and Change in Human Characteristics*—the result of his efforts to synthesize longitudinal studies of cognitive development during the previous 50 years. Bloom concluded that a large number of cognitive skills—especially verbal ability, so-called general intelligence, and school achievement—revealed a pattern of rapid development in the early years followed by a slower rate of development later. Perhaps his most influential claim was the assertion that by age 4, around 50% of the variation in cognitive skills possible for any particular child can be accounted for. Bloom (1964) concluded that early childhood education can profoundly affect "the child's general learning pattern" (p. 110).

The work of Hunt, Bloom, and others might well have been ignored had it not been for the social context surrounding their publications. Initiated by President Kennedy and continued by President Johnson, early childhood education quickly became an important component in the war against poverty. Late in 1964, a panel of pediatricians, child development researchers, educators, and psychologists recommended to the Office of Economic Opportunity (OEO) that preschool programs be implemented in order to help poor children develop to their full potential (Steiner, 1976, pp. 26–29; Zigler & Valentine, 1979). Proponents of compensatory education maintained that children in poverty lacked the kinds of experiences and opportunities available to children in more prosperous homes. Further, they declared that by the time poor children got to public school, they were too often already unable to take full advantage of the situation since their preschool years were deprived. Early compensatory education seemed once again to promise to break the cycle of poverty.

Early the next year, OEO acted on the recommendations of the panel and created Project Head Start. Motivated both by political considerations as well as a genuine concern about the effects of poverty on child development, Project Head Start sought to reach not only the "whole child," but parents and community as well. Efforts to improve the poor child's physical health as well as to foster cognitive, social, and emotional development led to programs that combined medical and psychological services with educational enrichment. Socialization efforts were made to increase the child's sense of dignity and self-worth as well as his or her capacity to relate positively to family and society. In addition to providing for child care and preschool education, Head Start programs sought to involve parents in such a way as to facilitate community organization and political action (Steiner, 1976, pp. 26–29; Zigler & Valentine, 1979).

Launched as a summer program in 1965, Head Start enrolled 561,359 poor children in 11,068 Head Start centers located in 1,398 communities. At the end of the summer, the administration decided to expand Head Start. That fall, 171,000 poor children from 3 to 6 years of age enrolled in a yearlong program of social and cognitive enrichment, medical care, and nutrition that has been called "the country's biggest peacetime mobilization of human resources and effort" (Payne et al., 1973, pp. 2–3).

Spinoffs from Head Start were not long in arriving. Home Start was created as an alternative—possibly more effective and less expensive—to Head Start. Parent and Child Centers were devised to teach parents about the health, developmental, and nutritional needs of their young children. Project Follow Through was initiated to carry over the benefits accrued from Head Start into the primary grades (Steiner, 1976, pp. 26–29). The guiding assumption and hope of these programs echoed earlier experiments in compensatory education. Proponents hoped that the cycle of poverty could be short-circuited through intensive work with poor families, especially among mothers and their young children.

A FINAL WORD

There is good child care and poor child care. These differences make differences in the child's experience and may affect later development. Historically, differences in quality of child care have been associated with differences in socioeconomic class.

As we enter into an era in which child care has, for the first time, become a widely discussed political issue, we must remain mindful of the historical persistence of a tiered system of child care and education. Like the poverty-track infant schools, the compensatory education programs of the 1960s and 1970s were established in the hope of ushering in social reform through pedagogical innovation. These efforts in compensatory education cannot, however, as Lazerson (1971) and others have reminded us, substitute for more structured kinds of economic reform for the poor. Finally, it may help to remember an ideal expressed some time ago by a true believer in democracy and education, John Dewey: "What the best and wisest parent wants for his own child, that must the community want for all its children. Any other ideal . . . destroys our democracy" (1916, p. 3).

REFERENCES

NOTE: Much of the factual information reported here was derived from two sources: Ilse Forest (1927), *Preschool education: A historical and critical study*, New York: Macmillan, 1927; and Robert M. Tank (1980), *Young children, families, and society in America since the 1820s: The evolution of health, education, and child care programs for preschool children*, doctoral dissertation, University of Michigan, Department of History. Many original sources as cited therein are cited below and, where possible, these primary sources have been verified.

Abbott, G. (1938). *The child and the state*. Chicago: University of Chicago Press.

Addams, J. (1910). *Twenty years at Hull-House*. New York: Macmillan.

Anonymous (1829). Infant education. (February.) *The Ladies Magazine, 2*, 89.

Anonymous (1902). The function of the day nursery. *Charities, 8*.

Anonymous (1914). The conservation of the home. *Outlook, 108*, 809–10.

Anonymous. (1918). Mushroom day nurseries checked. (November.) *The Survey*, 41.

Anonymous (1924). What day nurseries are doing. *Child Health Magazine, 5*.

Anonymous (1942). Eight hour orphans. (October.) *Saturday Evening Post*.

Anonymous (1945). Day care in October. *Bulletin of the Child Welfare League of America, 24*.

Anonymous (1946). National trends in day care. *Bulletin of the Child Welfare League of America, 25*.

Babcock, F. (1904). The aim of the day nursery. *American Motherhood, 19*.

Baker, J. (1919). Day nursery standards (U.S. Children's Bureau Bulletin No. 60). Washington, D.C.: U.S. Government Printing Office.

Baruch, B. (1943). *Journal of Consulting Psychology, 7*.

Beatty, B. R. (1981). *A vocation from on high: Preschool advocacy and teaching as an occupation for women in nineteenth-century Boston*. Unpublished doctoral dissertation, Harvard Graduate School of Education.

Beer, E. (1957). *Working mothers and the day nursery*. New York: Whiteside.

Bell, W. (1965). *Aid to dependent children*. New York: Columbia University Press.

Belsky, J. (1988). A reassessment of infant day care. In E.F. Zigler & M. Frank (Eds.), *The parental leave crisis: Toward a national policy (pp. 100-119)*. New Haven: Yale University Press.

Billingsley, A., & Giovannoni, J. M. (1972). *Children of the storm: Black children and American child welfare*. New York: Harcourt Brace Jovanovich.

Bloom, B. (1964). *Stability and change in human characteristics*. New York: Wiley.

Bond, E. (1945). Day care of children of working mothers in New York State during the war emergency. *New York History, 26*.

Bossard, A. (Ed.). (1940). Children in a depression decade. *Annals of the American Academy of Political and Social Science*. Philadelphia: American Academy of Political and Social Science.

Bowlby, J. (1951/1952). *Maternal care and mental health: a report prepared on behalf of the World Health Organization as a contribution to the United Nations program for the welfare of homeless children* (2nd ed.). Geneva: World Health Organization.

Brace, C. L. (1973). *The dangerous classes of New York, and twenty years' work among them.* Washington, D.C.: National Association of Social Workers (original work published 1872).

Bradbury, D. (1974). *The United States Children's Bureau, 1912–1972.* New York: Arno Press (original work, *Five decades of action for children: A history of the Children's Bureau,* published 1962).

Bremner, R. (1956). *From the depths: The discovery of poverty in the United States.* New York: New York University Press.

Brown, J. (1960). Child welfare classics. *Social Service Review, 34 (2),* 195-202.

Caldwell, G. (1919). Standards of admission to day nurseries. In *Proceedings of the National Conference of Social Work.* Chicago: National Conference of Social Work.

Cantrel, H. (1951). Public opinion, 1935-1946. Princeton, N.J.: Princeton University Press.

Chafe, W. H. (1972). *The American woman.* New York: Oxford University Press.

Child Welfare League of America. (1942). *Bulletin, 21.*

Cleveland Day Nursery and Free Kindergarten Association (1892). *Annual report.* Cleveland: Author.

Close, K. (1943). Day care up to now, *Survey Midmonthly, 79.*

Cochin, J. D. M. (1853). *Manuel des salles d'asile.* Paris.

Colbourne, F. (1924). Too near to be seen? *The Survey, 51.*

Conference of Day Nurseries (1892). *Report.* New York: Author.

Cravens, H. (1985). Child-saving in the age of professionalism, 1915–1930. In J. Hawes and N. Hiner (Eds.), *American childhood: A research guide and historical handbook.* Westport, Ct: Greenwood Press.

Cunningham, C., & Osborn, D. K. (1979). A historical examination of blacks in early childhood education. *Young Children, 35,* No. 3, March, 20–29.

Davis, M., & Hansen, R. (1933). *Nursery schools: Their development and current practices in the United States.* Washington, D.C.: U.S. Government Printing Office.

Department of Education, Commonwealth of Kentucky. (1936). *Educational Bulletin, 4.* Frankfort, Ky.: Author.

Devine, E. T. (1910). *The principles of relief.* New York: Macmillan.

Dewey, J. (1916). *Democracy and education.* New York: Macmillan.

Dewey, M. (1897). The scope of day nursery work. *Proceedings.* Boston: National Conference of Charities and Corrections.

Dodge, (Mrs.) A. (1897). The development of the day nursery. *Outlook, 56.*

Forest, I. (1927). *Preschool education: A historical and critical study.* New York: Macmillan.

Gamble, T., & Zigler, E. (1986). Effects of infant day care: Another look at the evidence. *American Journal of Orthopsychiatry, 56,* 26-41.

Griffin, M. K. (1906). The Hope Day Nursery. *The Colored American, 10 (5),* 397–400.

Grubb, W. N., & Lazerson, M. (1982). *Broken promises: How Americans fail their children.* New York: Basic Books.

Hartt, M. B. (1911). The day nursery problem. *Good Housekeeping, 52,* 22–23.

Hayes, C. (1916). *A political and social history of modern Europe.* New York: Macmillan.

Hedger, C. (1919). Standards of hygiene and equipment of day nurseries. In *National Conference of Social Work Proceedings.* Chicago: National Conference of Social Work.

Hidden, J. (1927). The Winsor Club nursery schools in Boston. *Childhood Education, 3.*

Hopkins, H. (1936). *Spending to save.* Seattle: University of Washington Press.

Hunt, J. M. (1961). *Intelligence and experience.* New York: Ronald Press.

Infant School Society of Boston (1828). *Constitution and by-laws.* Boston: T.R. Marvin.

Kelley, F. (1914). *Modern industry in relation to the family.* New York: Longmans.

Kuhn, A. (1947). *The mother's role in childhood education: New England concepts, 1830–1860.* New Haven: Yale University Press.

Lajewski, H. (1959). *Child care arrangements of full-time working mothers.* Washington, D.C.: U.S. Department of Health, Education and Welfare.

Langdon, G. (1938). Works Progress Administration emergency nursery school. *Progressive Education, 15.*

Lazerson, M. (1971). Urban reform and the schools: Kindergartens in Massachusetts, 1870–1915. *History of Education Quarterly, 11,* 115–142.

Leff, M. (1973). Consensus for reform: The mothers'-pension movement in the progressive era. *Social Service Review, 47,* 397–417.

Lerner, G. (1974). Early community work of Black club women. *Journal of Negro History, 59,* 158–167.

Lewinsky-Corwin, E. H. (1923). *Summary of findings of a report made for the New York Academy of Medicine* (n.p.).

Lomax, E. (1977). The LSRM: some of its contributions to early research in child development. *Journal of the History of the Behavioral Sciences, 13,* 283–293.

Lubove, R. (1965). *The professional altruist: The emergence of social work as a career, 1880–1930.* Cambridge: Harvard University Press.

Merrill Palmer School of Homemaking. (1921). *Second Annual Report.* Detroit, Mich.: Author.

Moustakas, C. E. and Berson, M. P. (1955). *The nursery school and child care center.* New York: Whiteside.

Myrdal, A. and Klein, V. (1968). *Women's two roles.* New York: Humanities Press.

National Advisory Committee on Emergency Nursery Schools. (1934). *Emergency nursery schools during the first year.* Washington, D.C.: Author.

National Advisory Committee on Emergency Nursery Schools. (1935). *Emergency nursery schools during the second year.* Washington, D.C.: Author.

National Conference on Day Nurseries. (1902, December). *Charities, 65.*

National Federation of Day Nurseries. (1922). *Report of the Conference.* New York: Author.

Nursery for the Children of Poor Women in the City of New York (1854). *Constitution, by-laws, and regulations.* New York: Author.

Payne, J. S., et al. (1973). *Head Start: a tragicomedy with epilogue.* New York: Behavioral Publications.

Proceedings of the conference on the care of dependent children held at Washington, D.C. (1909). Washington, D.C.: U.S. Government Printing Office.

Rosenau, N. S. (1894). Day nurseries. In National Conference of Charities and Correction, *Proceedings.* Boston: Author.

Rothman, S. (1973). Other people's children: The day care experience in America. *Public Interest, 30,* 11-27.

Ruderman, F. (1968). *Child care and working mothers.* New York: Child Welfare League of America.

Russell, W. F. (1931). The machine age and the future of the nursery school. *Childhood Education, 8.*

St. Agnes Day Nursery (1888). *Report.* New York: Author.

Scarr, A. (1984). *Mother care, other care.* New York: Basic Books.

Schlossman, S. (1981). Philanthropy and the gospel of child development. *History of Education Quarterly, 21,* 275–299.

Siegel, A. W., & White, S. H. (1982). The child study movement: Early growth and development of the symbolized child. *Advances in Child Development and Behavior, 17,* 233–285.

Smith, A. (1901). *The wealth of nations* (Vol. 1). London: Bell.

Spitz, R.A. (1945). Hospitalisation: An inquiry into the genesis of psychiatric conditions in early childhood. *The psychoanalytic study of the child, I.* New York: International Universities Press.

Spitz, R. (1946). Hospitalism: A follow-up report. *The psychoanalytic study of the child, II.* New York: International Universities Press.

Steiner, G. (1976). *The children's cause.* Washington, D.C.: The Brookings Institution; pp. 26–29.

Steinfels, M. (1973). *Who's minding the children? The history and politics of day care in America.* New York: Simon & Schuster.

Stoddard, G. (1934). Emergency nursery schools and child health. *Child Health Bulletin, 10.*

Tank, R. M. (1980). *Young children, families, and society in America since the 1820s: The evolution of health, education, and child care programs for preschool children.* (Doctoral dissertation, Department of History, University of Michigan, Ann Arbor). *University Microfilms International*, No. 8106233.

Tyson, H. G. (1924). *A study of day nurseries in Pennsylvania*. Harrisburg: Pennsylvania State Department of Public Welfare.

Tyson, H. G. (1925). *Day nurseries in Pennsylvania*. Harrisburg: Pennsylvania State Department of Public Welfare.

U. K., Lords. (1835). Speech made in the House of Lords on the education of the people, May 21, 1835. *Education in England*, Vol. 20, pp. 12f.

U.S. Congress, Senate, Committee on Education and Labor. (1943). *Hearings on the wartime care and protection of children of employed mothers*. 78th Congress, 1st session. Washington, D.C.: U.S. Government Printing Office.

Waller, W. (1945, February 18). The coming war on women. *This Week*.

Wetherill, G. (1943). *Hygeia, 21*, 634–635.

Whipple, G. (Ed.) (1929). *National Society for the Study of Education twenty-eighth yearbook: Preschool and parental education*. Bloomington, IL: Public School Publishing Co.

Whitbread, N. (1972). *The evolution of the nursery-infant school: A history of infant and nursery education in Britain, 1800-1870*. London: Routledge & Kegan Paul.

White, S. H., & Buka, S. (1987). Early education: Programs, traditions, and policies. In E.Z. Rothkopf (Ed.), *Review of research in education:* Vol. 14 (pp. 43–91). Washington, D.C.: American Educational Research Association.

White House Conference on Child Health and Protection. (1931). Section 4: The handicapped. Committee on socially handicapped. *A survey of day nurseries*. Washington, D.C.: Author.

Wilderspin, S. (1825). *Infant education: Remarks on the importance of educating the infant poor from the age of eighteen months to seven years* (3d ed.). London: J.S. Hodson.

Wolf, A. (1933). Nursery schools for the modern world. *The Public Health Nurse, 25*.

Woods, R., & Kennedy, A. (1922). *The settlement horizon..* New York: Russell Sage.

Woolley, H. (1926). The real function of the nursery school. *Child Study, 3*, 5.

Wright, H. (1922). *Children of wage-earning mothers: A selected group in Chicago* (Children's Bureau Publication No. 102). Washington, D.C.: Children's Bureau, U.S. Department of Labor.

Yates, J. S. (1905). Kindergartens and mothers' clubs as related to the work of the National Association of Colored Women. *The Colored American Magazine, 8*, 304–311.

Zigler, E., & Valentine, J. (Eds.). (1979). *Project Head Start: A legacy of the War on Poverty*. New York: Free Press.

BIOGRAPHICAL NOTES

Emily D. Cahan received her B.A. from Harvard University, magna cum laude, in 1978, and her Ph.D., in psychology, from Yale University in 1987. While at Yale, she was a Fellow at the Bush Center for Child Development and Social Policy. Her publications include *The First Fifty Years: The William T. Grant Foundation, 1936-1986*, and, with William Kessen, "A Century of Psychology: From Subject to Object to Agent" in *American Scientist*. Currently a Spencer Foundation Fellow of the National Academy of Education, she is working toward the publication of her dissertation on the origins of developmental psychology in 19th-century thought.

Bettye M. Caldwell, Ph.D., is Donaghey Distinguished Professor of Education at the University of Arkansas at Little Rock. Her professional career has had three major tracks—research, program development, and advocacy for children and families at the local, state, and national levels. In Syracuse, New York, she developed the first infant day care program in the United States. A major focus of her advocacy efforts has been to help gain professional and public acceptance of the concept that quality child care cannot be separated from quality education and that programs offering the best of both services are essential for children and families. Dr. Caldwell has published more than one hundred articles and books.

Judith E. Jones, M.S., is Director of the National Center for Children in Poverty and Associate Clinical Professor of Public Health at Columbia University, where she previously served as Deputy Director, Center for Population and Family Health. At the center she designed and managed a broad range of clinical and educational programs that facilitated community and institutional preventive strategies to assist underserved low-income women, adolescents, and children. Professor Jones has developed graduate courses at Columbia on health care program design and implementation, and she has authored numerous publications on adolescent health care, community health, and education programs. Among many committee appointments, she currently serves on the Committee on Child Development Research and Public Policy and the Steering Committee of the National Forum on the Future of Children and Their Families, National Academy of Sciences.

INDEX